MULTILINGUAL EUROPE
Diversity and Learning

*edited by Charmian Kenner
and Tina Hickey*

tb

Trentham Books
Stoke on Trent, UK and Sterling, USA

Trentham Books Limited
Westview House   22883 Quicksilver Drive
734 London Road   Sterling
Oakhill   VA 20166-2012
Stoke on Trent   USA
Staffordshire
England ST4 5NP

First published 2008

British Library Cataloguing-in-Publication Data
A catalogue record for this book is available from the British Library.

ISBN: 978 1 85856 423 4

The author and publisher wish to thank the following for their kind permission to reproduce material: Gibson Ferguson for Image 1; Miquel Tarradell School for Image 2; Grup d'Estudis Pedagògics for Image 3; Pollachi Nasan for Image 4; Wereld School Utrecht for Image 5; Christine Hélot for Images 6 and 11; Andrea Young for Image 7; Olga Barradas for Image 8; Kutlay Yagmur for Image 9; Claudine Kirsch for Image 10; CILT for Images 12, 13 and 14; The National Strategies for Image 15, Gildas Bernier for the diagram 'Learning connections'.

Cover photograph: with thanks to Albert Huber

Designed and typeset by Trentham Print Design Ltd, Chester and printed in Great Britain by Page Bros (Norwich) Ltd.

Contents

*This book is dedicated to everyone who participated
in the Multilingual Europe ESRC seminar series at Goldsmiths,
University of London, and to the children, parents and teachers
who have increased our funds of knowledge
by taking part in our research*

Introduction
Charmian Kenner and Tina Hickey

Multilingual Europe: hopes and challenges

What can educators across Europe learn from each other about successful multilingual initiatives? This book brings together the ideas and inspirations generated by a network of researchers, practitioners and policy makers from seven European countries. We are concerned to build learning communities in which children and young people can develop the skills needed to thrive in a multilingual society. All children have the right to become capable users of more than one language, by maintaining their existing languages and adding new ones. Our research shows that learning through different languages provides cognitive benefits, fosters multilingual identities and offers an understanding of other cultural worlds. This gives young people from diverse linguistic and cultural backgrounds the greatest chance of success.

Our shared vision represents a very different way forward from the climate of opinion currently expressed by some politicians and policy makers. In 2005, the Dutch minister for immigration campaigned – unsuccessfully – to stop languages other than Dutch from being spoken on the street. In 2008, she started a new political movement 'Proud of the Netherlands' that became immensely popular because of its anti-immigration stance. In France in 2004, the Bénisti report prepared for the government linked the speaking of a language other than French at home with juvenile delinquency and recommended that parents of children between the ages of 0 to 3 'of foreign origin ... should force themselves to speak French at home so that their children get used to having only this language to express themselves' (Bénisti, 2004:9). The report provoked an outcry and was later dropped. Meanwhile in the UK in 2006, a new headteacher at a London secondary school closed down bilingual classes designed to help children access the science curriculum through both Turkish and English, and received instant media support for her 'English only' policy.

1

Whilst some of these are extreme examples operating on an ideological level, they generate a climate of opinion that directly affects mainstream education. The global context of 'fear and blame of the other' allows for such ideas to be constructed, expressed, and sometimes legalised. Alternative discourses such as the Council of Europe's call for 'plurilingualism' in education (Beacco and Byram, 2003) struggle to be recognised. Even where a government department expresses some support for multilingualism at policy level – such as the UK National Languages Strategy promoting a variety of languages in the curriculum – other aspects of government policy in the same country may have a different rhetoric, such as anti-immigrant legislation. In most countries and settings, learning prestigious 'European' languages is considered to bring cognitive and cultural benefits, whilst 'indigenous minority' languages are largely ignored, and children speaking 'immigrant' languages are expected to have problems in school (Hélot, 2007). In the Netherlands, for example, 'bilingual education' automatically means teaching some subjects in Dutch and others in English, rather than involving a wider range of languages. Thus there are 'incoherent discourses' (Anderson *et al*, 2008) around multilingualism in education, reflecting the struggle between contradictory perspectives in the wider society.

This is therefore a particularly important time to draw strength from positive initiatives around Europe, and this book explores such initiatives. For example, we find the municipality of Utrecht funding significant numbers of multicultural projects, national policies in Sweden supporting bilingualism, a secondary school in Barcelona with a multilingual website hosted by its pupils, a primary school in France inviting parents to share languages and cultures, innovative multilingual literacy practices within the trilingual education system in Luxembourg, and nurseries in Ireland where young children can maintain Irish as a heritage language or learn it as a new language. By studying such examples in their social and political contexts, and considering their commonalities and differences, we can generate ideas relevant to our own educational environments. Comparative work involving critical reflection helps us to challenge our taken for granted perspectives.

Diversity and learning

The contributors to the book were participants in the Multilingual Europe seminar series hosted by Goldsmiths, University of London. Over a period of two years, this brought together researchers, practitioners and policy makers from seven European countries – France, Ireland, Luxembourg, the Netherlands, Spain, Sweden and the UK – plus a colleague from Israel whose work fosters bilingual and bicultural contact in a particularly challenging context through setting up Arabic/Hebrew bilingual schools.

The book does not seek to provide a comprehensive overview of policies and practices around Europe. That would be another book, for another purpose. Here we offer insights gained by bringing together case studies of progressive multilingual and multicultural projects. Neither do we aim to provide definitive answers to the complex questions posed by education in multilingual societies. Rather, we consider thought-provoking issues raised by our shared reflections, that can throw new light on ways forward within Europe and elsewhere. Our focus on diversity and learning involves learning *about* diversity – the myriad backgrounds from which multilingual pupils come – and learning *through* diversity, by finding out about different approaches to multilingualism in classrooms and communities.

Different contexts, different terminologies

One of the first things that struck us when we began our collaboration on multilingual research, policy and practice was the variation in the terms used in different countries when discussing this field. Every term has a history and a political statement behind it, which we need to unravel as we seek communication across boundaries. Given that each author in this book is writing from their own socio-political context and that the book will also be read in different countries, we have not tried to standardise terminology. We therefore ask readers to be aware that certain terms may be used in ways that differ from their usual experience.

It is important to be aware of the specific context in which each of the multilingual initiatives described here is taking place. Every European country has a different history of migration, due to its particular colonial links and labour requirements. For example, the UK relieved its postwar labour shortages by seeking workers from Commonwealth countries in South Asia and the Caribbean in the 1950s and 1960s (Edwards, 2004), whereas significant migration into Spain has only occurred since the mid-1990s, and is not only from Morocco but from around the world, as part of the new wave of global migration (Carrasco, 2004). The response of a post-war society to increasing linguistic and cultural diversity differs from that of a country experiencing globalisation at the start of the millennium.

Approaches to newly arrived communities in different European countries vary. In France, and increasingly in the Netherlands, new communities are encouraged to adapt to the host country's linguistic and cultural norms rather than retaining an 'ethnic minority' identity (Hélot, 2005). In contrast, in Sweden and the UK there is a policy discourse supporting ethnic and linguistic diversity in society and schools, though educational practice tends to remain monolingual (Axelsson, 2005; Kenner, 2004). Luxembourg is already trilingual and children become literate in all three languages, but there is a need to consider the status and role of other languages from children's home backgrounds (Portante, 2004). Meanwhile, Ireland and autonomous communities in Spain such as Catalonia may see the arrival of new linguistic groups as a challenge to their fragile indigenous languages, for example in terms of resource allocation or perceived national priorities (Castells, 2001; Council of Europe, 2008). Coming to terminology, the words 'foreigner' or 'immigrant' would now be seen in the UK as negative if applied to long-term residents. In Sweden, 'foreign' used to mean having one or both parents born outside Sweden but is now only used if both parents were born outside Sweden or the child was born outside the country. Changes in terminology can therefore be observed, depending on the history of immigration and settlement in each country.

A struggle over terminology in Ireland, a country where immigration is even more recent, has moved rapidly through a number of terms such as 'asylum-seekers' and 'non-nationals', rejecting each as they acquire negative connotations and opting currently for the terms 'foreign nationals,' 'new Irish' and, in the school context, 'international children'. Whilst the latter has positive overtones, being more often associated with children from a privileged business or diplomatic background, does it also suggest they are not expected to become a permanent part of Irish society? And does the term 'new Irish' focus on the assimilation of migrants in a melting pot model, rather than promoting integration in a mosaic model that values diversity?

Meanwhile, in southern European countries such as Spain, popular uses of 'foreigner' typically refer to the children of settled richer neighbours, while 'immigrant' is negatively associated with poorer non-nationals. Education authorities use the term 'newcomer pupils', which is intended to be more neutral but makes the richness of these children's diverse backgrounds invisible as soon as they learn Spanish or Catalan.

Thus terminology should not be taken at face value, since the meanings called up in one context may differ from those evoked in another. For example, 'black' and 'white' schools are terms used in the Netherlands which would be avoided in the UK context, where the nearest acceptable term would be 'mainly white' schools, even though schools also exist in the UK that

4

have mainly or entirely black or white populations. These are located in inner-city areas and are due largely to some white parents taking their children out of culturally mixed schools, a phenomenon often termed 'white flight'. Perhaps 'telling it like it is' can generate a clearer response, such as the World Schools project in Utrecht that arranges for schools with different pupil populations to visit each other and encourages interaction between pupils and parents.

One of the main issues encountered in international work is the search for a common term for 'community languages', 'minority languages', or 'immigrant languages'. The VALEUR project (McPake *et al*, 2007), researching provision of such languages across Europe, found it difficult to agree on a common naming system so circulated a questionnaire throughout the partnership for comment. 'Home languages' suggests a lack of relevance to the wider society, whilst 'heritage languages' or 'languages of origin' may be seen as looking towards the past rather than the future. 'Community languages' is a term often used in the UK, and may indicate that the existence of ethnic minority 'communities' is accepted and to some extent celebrated, even though a 'community' is notoriously difficult to define and is inevitably undergoing continual change and re-arrangement. 'Immigrant' would be seen as pejorative and marginalising in the UK, whilst 'minority' is more acceptable but less positive than 'community'. But 'community' is not widely used in other countries. In France, for example, *communauté* suggests division and splintering from mainstream society, often equated with a refusal to integrate and become a true citizen of the *République*. Eventually, the VALEUR project opted for the term 'additional languages', but no term was found to be entirely problem-free.

Finally, we find new terms constantly coming into play, such as 'plurilingual'. Some writers use this interchangeably with 'multilingual', whilst others use multilingual to refer to a society where a number of languages co-exist, and plurilingual to refer to the language knowledge of individuals within that society. The Council of Europe defines 'plurilingual competence' as 'a communicative competence to which all knowledge and experience of language contributes' (Beacco and Byram, 2003:4), in other words as a linguistic repertoire in which a person may have different levels of competence and different skills in each language, appropriate for their particular purpose. Such a definition allows for children's 'additional languages' to play a significant part as a resource. Given the variety of meanings currently emerging for these terms, we have not tried to standardise the use of 'plurilingual' or 'multilingual' by authors in this book.

How research, policy and practice interlink to promote multilingual education

Despite differences in context, history and terminology, common themes arise across European countries concerning new multilingual identities, language policy and planning, and school curricula appropriate to a multicultural population. To address these issues, we need to consider the three main types of action that influence success for multilingual education in Europe: research, policy and practice.

We begin this discussion by focusing on the value of *research* – which is too often marginalised or ignored. Research gives the opportunity for in-depth exploration of issues, asking questions and offering a critical perspective. We particularly support qualitative research, often ethnographic, and action research involving practitioners, rather than the statistical data usually required by policymakers. Such localised studies reveal complexity and highlight the need to look for different responses in different contexts rather than the 'one size fits all' approach that governments tend to seek.

The role of *policy* is to give direction, vision and leadership, taking into account the findings of cutting-edge research. On-the-ground projects depend on policy validation for long-term success. We need policy that fosters the development of young people's multilingual skills and identities as a genuine investment in the future, instead of short-term initiatives oriented only towards employability.

Finally, *practice* is the key. It is the locus where people from different communities and backgrounds meet and interact. Practice develops responses to immediate needs, and shapes new forms of relationship and activity. It links with research, especially through practitioner reflection and action research, and generates significant findings that can nourish new policy debates.

Policy and practice which together relate closely to research give the greatest chance for success and build the strongest way forward. We discovered some examples that can inspire similar collaborations elsewhere:

- ■ In Sweden, the government gave money to local councils for initiatives on language development, with the proviso that a certain percentage was to be spent on evaluation through research. Councils quickly had to seek the involvement of researchers, who fed back a theoretical critique as well as empirical evidence, for example concerning in-service teacher training on bilingual learning. The researchers' findings were well received, even though they questioned policy, with policy makers' interest going beyond the evaluation process to engage with the theoretical issues raised.

- In the Netherlands, the municipality of Utrecht asked university researchers to find out how well their policy initiatives for minority communities were working. The research highlighted the need to promote positive aspects of diversity, rather than seeing it as a problem. The Municipality then prepared an Interculturalisation Integration Policy, which included subsidies for intercultural activities in education, welfare, sport and the arts.

- In Spain, a consortium consisting of the City Council of Barcelona plus three universities set up the 'Observatory of Childhood' (CIIMU). This organisation conducts research and links researchers and policymakers. Studies have focused on areas such as multicultural education, family, health and the use of information technology. The results become part of a report published every two years on emerging issues and the evaluation of public policies in relation to children, families and social change.

- In the UK, bilingualism in schools is now supported by government policy at a rhetorical level, for example through statements acknowledging the value of first languages in learning. However, few examples are given of good practice, leaving practitioners unsure how to proceed. Action research linked with a particular policy initiative (the English as an Additional Language pilot programme) investigated ways of putting bilingual learning into practice for children of second and third generation Bangladeshi heritage in schools in East London. Results were fed back to policymakers via a dissemination conference. Meanwhile the pilot programme had developed useful materials on first language use in schools – which now need additions that will take the needs of these children into account.

- In France, researchers took part in a European project called TESSLA, Teacher Education for the Support of Second Language Acquisition (www.tessla.org). Together with colleagues from Edinburgh University they developed curricula for initial teacher education that would prepare future primary teachers to support children who are acquiring a second language. Through a dissemination conference, local policy makers and administrative staff became convinced of the need to include such issues in the initial education of all mainstream teachers.

This book itself represents an innovative collaboration across boundaries between practitioners, researchers and policy makers. That process made a
significant contribution to the knowledge and development of all who took
part. Meeting the needs of multilingual Europe requires the sharing of ideas
and information between countries, a necessary and valuable part of ongoing
professional development. Such cooperation plays a significant part in
heightening awareness of the wider issues relating to multilingualism, and
promoting discussion of how the insights from other countries might relate
to our own context. This is illustrated by a selection of comments from participants in the Multilingual Europe seminar series. We have retained the
original language (French, Spanish/Catalan, Swedish, Turkish and Dutch) in
order to give a flavour of the multilingual exchange.

*'Chaque séminaire fut une source d'inspiration et motivation pour mon travail de
recherche dans le domaine du plurilinguisme en France. Une véritable fenêtre
ouverte sur l'Europe.'*

*'Participar en los seminarios ha sido un privilegio para aprender de distintas
experiencias y disciplinas, pero sobre todo, con personas entusiastas, cercanas
y comprometidas ... amb totes les llengües i les persones que les parlem.'*

*'Seminarierna gav mig möjlighet att få ta del av och jämföra arbetssätt och
attityder till flerspråkighet i Europa som kommer att ha betydelse för Sveriges
fortsatta arbete med flerspråkiga barn.'*

*'Seminerler ve öğrenme sürecinde diğer dillerin görünürlüğünü sağlayarak
sınırları zorlamakta ısrar edenler, ortak bir ilham kaynağı vahası yaratarak yeni
ufuklar açtılar.'*

*'De bijeenkomsten waren een verademing door de eensgezindheid en het
optimisme van de deelnemers. In tegenstelling tot hoe het in Nederland (en
elders) vaak gaat hoefde je hier niet eerst uit te leggen dat meertaligheid iets
goeds is. Dat maakte dat er tijd en aandacht was om vanuit een gedeelde
achtergrondvisie ter zake te komen!'*

Overview of the book

The three parts of the book consider:

- how identities are constructed in multilingual contexts
- how schools can link with families and communities
- how educational systems, policies and practices can support innovative pedagogies for multilingual classrooms

Each part begins with a theoretical overview, leading on to chapters that present material from the seminar series on a particular theme. The conclusion to each part reflects on similarities and differences between projects and contexts, and suggests ways forward.

Identity plays a key role in educational achievement, since it involves children's sense of themselves as members of particular communities and as learners. Part One, **Understanding Identity in Multilingual Contexts**, explores the identities that emerge for children and young people growing up in multilingual cities such as Barcelona, Utrecht and Sheffield. Through the example of the world-wide Tamil community, it also examines how diasporic identities can be continually re-negotiated through the use of new media. The role of creativity in constructing identities is discussed through projects ranging from carnival in London schools and bilingual drama with young people of Bosnian heritage, to digital photography that brings together communities of different cultural backgrounds in a village in North Cyprus.

Schools flourish when they are integrally connected to the families and communities from which their pupils come. Part Two, **Home, School and Community**, explores the concept of a 'learning community' at different levels by examining home-school links in a project with grandparents in East London, links between schools in the same city in Utrecht, and links between teachers across Europe in an intercultural project on children's literature. Connections between schools and families are further discussed through research and practice in French primary schools, Swedish pre-schools and secondary schools in the Netherlands. The importance of community-run language initiatives in extending and complementing children's learning is demonstrated by classes run during school time, after school or at weekends by Portuguese, Chinese, South Asian and Turkish communities in the Netherlands and the UK.

Pedagogies to support language learning and overall educational achievement need to be adapted to the contexts and communities from which children and young people come. Part Three, **Learners, Teachers and Schools**, addresses this complexity by looking at innovative bilingual and multilingual models in situations as varied as trilingual Luxembourg, indigenous language maintenance in Ireland, pre-school education in the UK, and schools in Israel which bring together Arabic speaking and Hebrew speaking children. New developments in teacher education around Europe are presented, to support both mainstream and community schooling. Finally, the role of policymakers is considered by comparing provision for learning different languages across Europe, discussing new forms of assessment, and reflecting on what policies are needed to ensure that children from all backgrounds have opportunities to develop a rich and diversified plurilingual repertoire that will enhance their educational achievement.

To conclude, we offer a number of discussion points to stimulate reflection on the material contained in the book.

Part 1
Understanding identity in multilingual communities

Section editors: Jean Conteh and Aura Mor-Sommerfeld

Overview of Part 1

Conceptualisations of identity are now many and complex, taking us beyond the traditional view of it as a set of individual – albeit sociologically determined – attributes. This is important for understanding the ways in which identity influences individual and social action, particularly in multilingual communities. Holland and Lave (2001) argue that 'identities are always in process', 'unfinished' (p.9), 'historical' and often – of particular relevance to multilingual and diasporic communities – 'contested in practice' (p.6). Bhavnani and Phoenix (1994:9) suggest the illuminating metaphor of identity as 'a place from which the individual can express the multiple and often contradictory aspects of her/himself'. The metaphor of identity as a traveller, something which '... travels, but is about belonging' (Woodward, 2002:168), also reflects some of the contradictions, but it is a hopeful and enlightening idea to take with us as we move through the first two chapters of this book.

Identity, particularly in multilingual communities, needs to be understood as multi-layered, as socially, culturally and politically constructed, as potentially conflicted (Meinhof and Galasinski, 2005) and mediated. We argue that such a concept has a vital role to play in understanding and researching education, making an important contribution to theories of learning as a socio-cultural, meaning-making activity. In wider terms, it can also reveal the interplay between the local and the global in individual experiences and narratives (Meinhof and Galasinski, 2005), and help us recognise the effects of socio-political and economic influences on people's lives. However, a theory of identity must also include the notion of individual agency along with the idea of collective solidarity. Multilingual communities often need a strong sense of collective solidarity for social and political action and mutual support, while at the same time needing to offer a 'third space' (Bhabha, 1994) in which their members – particularly the younger generations – can express their individuality and creativity.

The complex and sometimes contradictory associations among identity, language and culture have been recognised for some time, and are becoming well-documented in research and writing (e.g. Tabouret-Keller, 1998; Mills, 2005). Studies of classroom interaction in linguistically and ethnically diverse settings (e.g. Heath, 1983; Nieto, 1999) have long revealed the ways in which language and culture are inextricably intermingled. Cole (1985) and other cultural psychologists recognise the ways in which the individual and the social come together in classroom conversations, and how 'culture and cognition create each other' (Cole, 1985:147), suggesting that the negotiation of identities is a crucial aspect of these conversations. Teachers and learners are therefore not simply transacting and co-constructing knowledge through their interactions, but also negotiating their personal and cultural identities.

This section of the book demonstrates the importance of understanding identity as a vital and central dimension of education in multilingual communities, and not just in classrooms. It explores identity construction in various contexts in Europe, illustrating social and cultural interaction in different layers of experience – from global to local – all ultimately linked to education. The first chapter focuses on how identities are reproduced and changed through the histories and development of communities in multilingual cities. The second considers how young people take advantage of opportunities to construct their own identities in different ways through narratives and creative action. Commonalities are thus revealed in the processes of identity construction at these different levels, all of which might have remained hidden if the chapters had been constructed only in a linear way. The thematic approach also helps to illuminate the key argument that understanding identity is crucial to understanding education in multilingual contexts.

We believe that thinking about identity and education is moved forward by the examples presented in the chapters that reveal the importance of community action and responsibility, and of creativity and representation in multilingual communities. These ways of learning have perhaps been regarded as peripheral in mainstream education. We argue that they should be seen as central, as facets of the powerful desire to make meaning, from which learning comes. Members of the multilingual communities described in these chapters have been working in different ways to construct a sense of belonging in the societies in which they live. In doing so, they derive strength from their *roots* while shaping their own ways forward – their own *routes* to community harmony and security.

1

Communities and identities in multilingual cities

This chapter presents four case studies of multilingual communities in Europe: the cities of Utrecht, Sheffield and Barcelona, and the Tamil diasporic community. The authors describe the rich diversity of detail in each setting and show strong common themes connecting the contexts, revealing the diverse ways in which community members negotiate and construct their identities and simultaneously maintain their social and communal links and values. The whole chapter provides an overview of the influence of historical, economic and sociopolitical events on identity construction in multilingual communities.

The Netherlands and Utrecht

Jacomine Nortier, University of Utrecht

Utrecht is situated in the middle of the Netherlands, not far from the other major cities in the western part of the country (Amsterdam, Rotterdam and Den Haag). It is the centre of a spider's web of roads and railways. With its many university and college students, it has a relatively young population.

In the 1960s and 1970s, when labour was badly needed in the Netherlands, factories and companies in Utrecht and elsewhere brought in unskilled guest workers from southern European countries such as Spain, Italy and Greece. Some of these workers stayed, whilst others returned to their home countries after several years of work. The largest groups of guest workers in Utrecht, however, were Moroccan or Turkish. Although their intention was to return home within a few years, the majority stayed in Utrecht and their families joined them, as happened in other western European cities. Over half (55-

60%) of the people in the Netherlands with Moroccan or Turkish backgrounds were born outside the country, the so-called first generation of migrants. The remaining 40-45%, the second and third generations, were born in the Netherlands. A relatively large proportion of the new arrivals are aged 20 to 40, because it has become popular among Moroccan and Turkish people to find marriage partners in their country of origin and 'marry them into the Netherlands'. This assures them of a safe future as social safety nets and health care are much more reliable in Holland than in their countries of origin.

Demographic background

In January 2006, there were a total of 16,334,210 people living in the Netherlands, of whom 19.3% had a non-native background. In Utrecht, the fourth largest city in the country with almost 281,000 inhabitants, this percentage was 30.7%. In the Netherlands, use of the word 'foreigner' is outdated, and the word 'migrant' is not yet very widespread. Instead, native Dutch people are called 'autochtones' and non-natives are talked about as 'allochtones'. In practice, the term 'allochtones' tends more and more to be used exclusively for people with non-western backgrounds.

Table 1.1 gives an overview of the distribution of some ethnic groups in the Netherlands and in the city of Utrecht. The proportionally largest non-western groups are included: people from Morocco (who are the main focus of this

Table 1.1: Population Statistics for The Netherlands and Utrecht in January 2006[1]

	Netherlands	Relative %	Utrecht	Relative %
Total population	16 334 210	100	280 949	100
Native Dutch	13 186 595	81.7	194 582	69.3
Non-native	3 147 615	19.3	86 367	30.7
Western	1 427 565	8.7	27 845	9.9
Non-Western	1 720 050	10.6	58 522	20.8
Morocco	323 239	1.98	24 667	8.8
Dutch Antilles and Aruba	129 683	0.8	2 276	0.8
Surinam	331 890	2.03	7 198	2.6
Turkey	364 333	2.23	12 656	4.5
Other non-Western	570 905	3.5	11 725	4.2

1. Based on www.cbs.nl

piece), Turkey, the Antilles and Surinam. The latter came because of former colonial ties – the country became independent from the Netherlands in 1975. Of course, groups are not evenly spread over the country. In Amsterdam and The Hague, for example, there is a relatively large number of people with a Surinamese background, whilst in Utrecht the largest group is Moroccans.

Ethnic tensions and integration

Within Utrecht, some areas are mainly Dutch while others have a more mixed population. In some areas of the city, the majority of the population is Moroccan. In particular in Kanaleneiland, in south-west Utrecht, the per- centage of people of Dutch origin is less than 15% in some parts. In this area, there have been tensions that were reported in the national media. Groups of Moroccan boys and young men took control of the streets; bus drivers, frightened by youths throwing stones, refused to drive through the heart of the area. Recently, journalists who wanted to report on the situation were attacked. One of the measures taken by the municipality to deal with the situation in the second half of 2007 was to prohibit large groups from assembling. However, not everyone agreed that this would solve the problem. At the same time, work was done on different types of solutions such as changing the dead-end situation in which many young Moroccans find themselves. Though Kanaleneiland has gained a reputation as a sometimes dangerous and difficult area, other people see the melting pot of cultures and ethnicities in Kanaleneiland as an exciting challenge. To avoid an escalation of the situation in Kanaleneiland and in other areas, the municipality has developed an active policy of integration.

From 1998 until 2001, I participated in a large-scale research project on the mixing of languages and cultures in Lombok-Transvaal, another area in Utrecht with a long-standing multi-ethnic history. One of the reasons for situating this project in Lombok-Transvaal was the successful and relatively peaceful coexistence there of people from many different ethnic back- grounds, which might serve as an example to people elsewhere. One of the things learned from the project was that integration in the most idealistic sense is not possible. Just as people from different social classes do not easily mix at all levels of life, people from different ethnic backgrounds, particularly first generation migrants, do not let outsiders into their lives at all levels. We observed, however, that people are able to live peacefully side by side and sometimes join each other for common activities. This type of coexistence may be the best that can be achieved. Compared to the situation in areas like Kanaleneiland, life in Lombok-Transvaal is much more peaceful.

Utrecht's policy on integration, interculturalisation and diversity

Within the municipality of Utrecht, an active policy called 'Diversity and Integration' has been developed to promote multicultural activities. The goals are to encourage social and cultural renewal, to fight all forms of deprivation, and to facilitate encounters between native and non-native citizens so that they can participate in a bidirectional form of integration called *intercultura-lisation*. To achieve these goals, large and smaller projects have been developed, some of which are presented below. Compared with other muni-cipalities in the Netherlands, the Utrecht policy has had a positive and stimu-lating effect on activities that promote multicultural togetherness. ➡ *see also Part 2: World schools p72 and Every parent counts p81.*

Local projects have been encouraged by prizes that offer a substantial amount of money. One of these is the bi-annual Utrecht Safety Award (*Utrechtse Veiligheidsprijs*). In 2005 this prize was won by a group that assists young refugees without family support when they reach their eighteenth birthday and their legal position changes. In another project that was nominated, a group who had previously been seen as causing problems in their neighbourhood, mainly consisting of young Moroccans, were given work in a recently opened local supermarket. Most of them now have jobs and positive prospects for the future. Among the projects nominated in 2007 is the work of a group of young people who organise intergenerational activi-ties for younger and older people in order to encourage a feeling of safety, social cohesion and togetherness in a problematic neighbourhood.

In another neighbourhood, which suffered from a group of noisy and aggres-sive teenagers, mothers organised activities in which the teenagers were en-couraged to work in the parks where they helped to make paving stones with their personal signatures. This put an end to a situation in which people felt powerless and angry. Another prize is the annual Tolerance Award. This was won in 1999 by three schools for their positive initiatives for tolerance within their school populations and the stimulating influence they had on life outside the schools. In 2006 the prize was awarded to a group that brought to-gether local citizens and people from a centre for asylum seekers.

Since 2002, there has been a 'Cultural Sunday' once every month, often with a theme that fits within the interculturalisation policy. During a full Sunday a large number of cultural institutes, museums, galleries and theatres open their doors to the public and organise free activities such as exhibitions and lectures that fit within a central theme. Examples of such themes are Museums for Children, Morocco, Turkey Express, Passion for Easter, Opera,

Dance, Story Telling and Enlightenment. World Celebration is an annually re-curring theme especially dedicated to interculturalisation.

Language issues

The local government provides language education as part of services that address the economic and social needs arising from migration. For example, courses where people learn how to become Dutch citizens (*inburgeringscur-sussen*) are organised for the so-called 'newcomers'. Here people learn how Dutch society is organised, where to go and what to do. Dutch language courses are also taught. In the earliest stages, instruction is sometimes given in the original language of the newcomer to help the learning of Dutch. The *inburgeringscursussen* are compulsory for newly-arrived migrants. The situation is more difficult for so-called 'oldcomers', people who have been living in Utrecht for years but never learned adequate Dutch, for whatever reason. Since 1999 they too have been offered language courses, but it is not easy to reach them. All educational activities sponsored by the government and municipality are directed towards the learning of Dutch. Multilingual prac-tices are not encouraged.

There are bilingual schools in the secondary school sector in Utrecht, as in other Dutch cities. These popular schools offer part of their lessons only in English. Established bilingualism in the Netherlands does not include lan-guages other than Dutch and English.

The government provided mother tongue education until August 2004, but this has never developed into a broadly accepted educational activity. There has been increasing resistance to this so-called 'waste of time', particularly since – as it is perceived – the children could have spent their time learning Dutch during those hours. For the past few years, the main goal of language teaching in primary education has been to learn Dutch, which, so it is thought, no longer leaves room for mother tongue teaching. ➡ *see also Part 2: Turkish community action in the Netherlands p110.*

In spite of this official policy, Harry Blume, director of the *Lukasschool* in Utrecht, Kanaleneiland, a primary school where the vast majority of pupils are of Moroccan heritage, decided with his staff to continue mother tongue teaching. Blume's positive and optimistic view concerning the situation of children of Moroccan origin is refreshing. Moroccan children are commonly associated with deprivation and with language problems that last beyond their primary school careers. Blume considers not only the level they reach by the time they leave primary school at the age of 12, but compares it to the level at which they entered school eight years earlier. Through this comparison, a strong improvement is visible.

The abolition of mother tongue teaching was a disaster for many teachers, who lost their jobs. At the *Lukasschool*, however, most mother tongue teachers were able to stay, partly because they were re-trained at an early stage, and partly because mother tongue teaching continued, though in a somewhat different form. The mother tongue is now used to facilitate and support the learning of Dutch.

How does this work in practice? There is continuous contact between the teachers of first language and the regular teachers, for example about words and concepts that turn out to be difficult or problematic during regular classes. With the help of the pupils' first language, both vocabulary and general knowledge are enlarged, extended and deepened. As the children move up into higher grades, the focus is not only on the technicalities of reading but also on the understanding of informative content, and independent reading strategies become more central. The results of including first language in the regular curriculum are promising. This approach leads to significantly higher results on the standardised tests that children take at the end of their primary school career. ➡ *see also Part 2: Bilingual teachers as agents of social change p104*.

Although the Dutch-only policy is strong, both in people's minds and in political circles, my hope for the future is that the Lukasschool's example will be followed by other schools in Utrecht and the rest of the country.

Multilingual Sheffield
Gibson Ferguson, University of Sheffield

A defining characteristic of the contemporary British city is its ethnic and cultural diversity and therefore its multilingualism. Sheffield, in south Yorkshire, is no exception, with 93 languages recorded as home languages by young people in its schools in 2007.

Sheffield is the fourth largest city in England, and like other cities in the English midlands and the north, continues to undergo transformation from an industrial past to a post-industrial present and future. Sheffield is world famous for steelmaking and this brought in workers from overseas in the 1950s and 1960s, notably the Pakistani/Kashmiri and Yemeni communities. Other communities, in particular the Somali community, have arrived as the result of civil war. More recently, people have arrived from the 'new accession' EU countries of Eastern Europe.

The population of Sheffield is over half a million. In some parts of the city, the minority population reaches over 70%, though in the affluent southwest it is less than 10%. Diverse as Sheffield is, the total ethnic minority population is not particularly high when compared with other post-industrial cities such as Birmingham. The most recent estimate, in 2006, puts the percentage at about 70,000 people, or 14%. However, this figure is a significant increase on the 2001 census count, which was just over 45,000 (nearly 9%). The percentages of ethnic minority entrants into primary school and of births are even higher, at 24% and 28% respectively. Sheffield's diversity is becoming an increasingly important and visible feature of city life.

Languages and communities in Sheffield

Of the 93 languages mentioned above, the great majority have only a handful of speakers, and just three – Panjabi, Urdu and Arabic – have more than a thousand speakers across the school sector. Many of those reporting themselves as Urdu speakers also speak a variety of Panjabi at home. Urdu has considerable prestige in the Pakistani community as the national language of Pakistan and, importantly, as the community language of literacy. Most of the Arabic speakers are Yemenis, and their community in Sheffield will be described in more detail below. The next largest community is Somali, and then come the Bengali speakers.

Four languages are recognised by the City Council in its literature and in some of its public signage: Arabic, Bengali, Chinese and Urdu. The Chinese com-

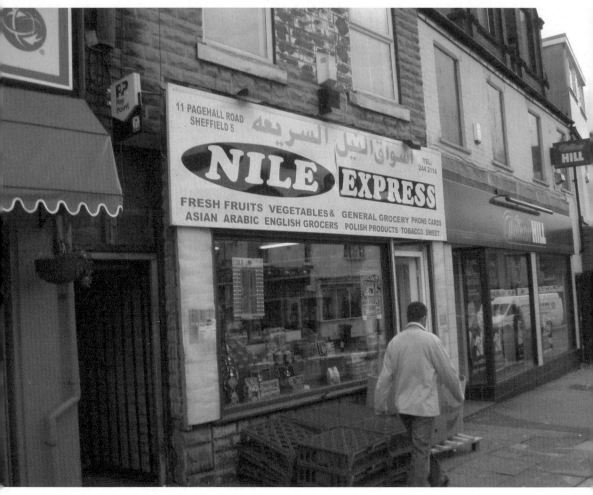

1.Shop in Firth Park, Sheffield, catering for older and newer language communities.

munity has an active Chinese Community Centre and supermarkets and restaurants in an area near the city centre, where there has been some talk of creating a Sheffield 'Chinatown'. The community runs two complementary schools to support children's learning of Chinese. The Bengali community's main centre of activity is the Bengali Women's Support Group. Led by poet and writer Debjani Chatterjee, they have published a number of enterprising bilingual books in Bengali and English, including a collection of recipes and poems, and a book called *A Slice of Sheffield* that celebrates the cutlery making for which the city is famous.

By far the largest ethnic minority community in Sheffield is the Pakistani one. The majority of the community arrived from rural areas in the 1950s and 60s, and had received little education in Pakistan. This meant that not many were Urdu speakers, and few would therefore be literate in a community language. The Pakistani community is active and visible in the city, with some large, well-established and influential community organisations. In the last year, the community has opened Sheffield's most recent landmark building, the Wolseley Road Mosque, with prominent green domes and two tall minaret towers.

There is also a flourishing transnational economic flow among the Pakistani community, with a triangle of trade between the Darnall area of Sheffield, Manchester (as the point of entry of goods by air) and Pakistan. This trade is carried on by family-run shopkeepers and focuses on the import and sale of foods such as mangoes, chillies and rice, and textiles. One of the largest traders in the latter is Karachi Stores, a department store. This business also hosts a radio station, 'Radio Ramadhan' which broadcasts in Urdu during the month of Ramadhan. The national bilingual Urdu-English newspaper *Jang* circulates widely in culturally diverse areas of the city and has reporters who are based locally.

Radio Sheffield broadcasts in a number of community languages, including Urdu, hooking up with the BBC Asian network for much of its programming. Other community languages broadcast locally are Arabic, Bengali, Chinese and Somali. The Somali community is the fastest growing minority community in the city. It has two active community centres, and a couple of complementary schools.

Promoting multilingualism in Sheffield

Sheffield has taken definite action to recognise and promote its multilingualism. The two organisations that have led this action are the Association of Sheffield Community Language Schools (ASCLS) and the MultiLingual City Forum (MLCF). They have recently merged to form Languages Sheffield, in order to provide a stronger voice across the city for languages and language learning.

The founding aims of the MultiLingual City Forum include 'to promote and extend existing bilingualism' and 'to encourage lifelong language learning'. It works with the local authority's educational services, and actively promotes language learning in schools. It also works with the Regional Language Network in Yorkshire and the Humber on matters of languages in business. One of its products has been the Sheffield City Languages Strategy, which was launched in March 2004, after twelve months' preparation by a partnership group that covered all sectors of education, including both the city's universities, business, the Learning and Skills Council, the Workers Educational Association (adult education) and Sheffield's Library and Information Service. Sheffield, together with Leicester city and county, are the only major cities in the UK with a languages strategy of this kind. In Sheffield the strategy is being monitored by the cross-sectoral Sheffield Languages Alliance, which is chaired by MLCF.

The Sheffield Languages Strategy aims to build further on the national strategy for England *Languages for All: Languages for Life.* ➡ *see also Part 3: The English National Languages Strategy p170.* First of all, the Sheffield strategy's scope is city-wide, across sectors, and not just education, although that is the most developed component and the one where the most obvious progress has been made. Second, it extends the entitlement to language learning from the age of seven, as in the national strategy, to the nursery and early years sector. Third, there is a greater emphasis on the role of community languages and their promotion, use and learning, than in the national strategy. Finally, the strategy includes a practical business-education linkage, the Vocational International Project Sheffield (VIPS) which now involves nearly all the secondary schools in the city and several hundred young people aged 15-16. The project involves local businesses as mentors, and hands-on language practice in the workplace, such as sending emails, making phone calls, and arranging meetings. VIPS has become nationally known and acknowledged, and has been taken up by some authorities outside Sheffield, one as far away as Cornwall.

As a result of these activities, Sheffield is being profiled by the Council of Europe's Language Policy Division, the first such profile of an individual city in Europe: to date such profiles have been of nations (eg Austria) or regions (eg Lombardy).

The second organisation fostering multilingualism in Sheffield is the Association of Sheffield Community Language Schools (ASCLS), an umbrella organisation for over 30 complementary schools that embrace seventeen languages. There is more than one school for Arabic, Bengali, Somali and Urdu, and at least one for the other languages which include Farsi, Malay, Chilean Spanish, Polish, Greek and Portuguese. One of the most valuable services provided by ASCLS is recognised training for volunteer teachers to develop language teaching that begins to match standards in mainstream schools.

Another activity has been working in four primary schools to support the teaching of Bengali, Somali and Urdu.

By 2006, Arabic and Urdu were offered at GCSE (the national examinations that are usually taken at age 16) in twelve of the city's 27 secondary schools, and in the further education institution, Sheffield College. Chinese was taken in eight schools and at Sheffield College. Other languages, offered in just one or two schools in each case, were Bengali, Farsi, Portuguese, Polish and Turkish. The number of young people taking Arabic is rising steadily year by year and it is now the fifth most popular language. However, although Urdu is the fourth most frequently taken language subject in Sheffield at GCSE after French, German and Spanish, with an average of almost 140 a year over 2001-2006, this still represents less than half of the students of Pakistani origin in the GCSE year.

The under-achievement of Somalis, as compared with the school perfor-mance of other minority communities in Sheffield's secondary schools, is a cause of official concern. Until the recent advent of the Asset Languages Ladder assessment system, there was no officially recognised public examination in Somali, and that has had a deleterious effect on the main-tenance of the language. The inclusion of Somali from September 2006 will hopefully boost the prestige of the language in the eyes of both Somalis and the wider community. ➡ *see also Part 3: The Languages Ladder and Asset Languages p175.*

The organisations and activities described above are an important part of Sheffield's response to the realisation, and the celebration, of its developing diversity. They are part of the efforts that continue to be needed, perhaps more urgently than ever, to inculcate a sense of multilingualism and multi-culturalism as a resource, not as a problem. The following section focuses on one of Sheffield's oldest ethnic minority communities, the Yemenis.

Yemenis in Sheffield:
A vignette of a diasporic community
Gibson Ferguson, University of Sheffield

The first Yemeni migrants arrived in Sheffield in the 1950s to take up employment in the steel industry. At its peak it is estimated that there were more than 8,000 people in the Yemeni community (Halliday 1992). With the decline of the steel industry, the community has contracted to around 3,000 to 4,000 thousand, comprising second and third generation descendants of the original migrants as well as a more recent wave of people joining their families, economic and political refugees displaced by the 1994 civil war in the Yemen, and asylum seekers.

A sizeable proportion of the community is UK born and schooled, often with limited or waning Arabic language skills. By contrast, recent incomers, as well as older men and women, have little English, the men because their English language proficiency is restricted to work-related functions and the women because of limited social and economic mobility. Lack of English is a considerable obstacle to accessing employment opportunities, medical and housing services and it impedes communication with schools. Older family members often visit the doctor, for example, with a child or relative as interpreter.

Adult classes in English as a second language provided by Sheffield College and other agencies are therefore popular, especially with women, and are seen as important for widening opportunities. There is concern about the potential cuts in government funding for these classes.

The following extracts from interviews carried out in Arabic by Laila Makdid show common patterns of language use in the Yemeni community. All names are pseudonyms.

Laila is a 38-year-old Yemeni woman who came to Sheffield with her husband and children as refugees in 2000. She has three children aged 16, 14, and 6, the youngest being born in the UK. Her husband is unemployed. She attends classes at the Yemeni Centre to improve her English, and also enjoys the social contacts the classes facilitate.

I can speak, write and read Arabic. My writing skill in English is good. I can read simple texts in English. I cannot read long words. I speak Arabic with my husband.

When my children speak in English at home I get annoyed and ask them to speak in Arabic in order for my youngest son to get used to Arabic and not forget it. My children speak with each other in English ... I prefer to speak in Arabic because I cannot speak in English very well. Even when I speak in English I feel embarrassed. I don't go out much to practise ... I watch Arabic TV programmes. My children watch English ones only ... I hope they don't forget their native language beside their English, which is essential here. Arabic is essential for going to Arabic countries.

Saleh is a 33-year-old Yemeni man who came to England in 2001 as a political refugee and was joined two years later by his wife and children (two girls and one boy – aged 8, 6 and 3). He is currently unemployed and, like Laila, attends English classes at the Yemeni Centre.

We have Arab friends. I speak with them in Arabic most of the time. Outside the house we speak in Arabic. In my community there are Arab people. Even at the shop where I go shopping for food the shopkeeper is Arab ... We watch Arabic channels on TV a lot. My wife watches Arabic and English. We like to watch 'Dr Who'. We watch it subtitled in Arabic on an Arabic channel.

[Yemeni people] must keep their language because it's their first language ... If they learned English it's good for them also. When you speak two languages it's good, even three or four languages. That's very good. You can go anywhere and have any job. You can help people who can't speak the language. You can translate and interpret for them.

We see a trend of language shift to English over the generations, which leads to complex patterns of intra-family communication. At the same time, we see the importance of satellite TV and Arabic broadcasting in the lives of many Yemeni families, which probably helps sustain the community's strong sense of its Arabic heritage. The interviews showed that Arabic continues to be highly valued, for its religious significance as the language of the Qur'an, as an identity marker, and for communicating with relatives and friends back in the Yemen. There is also a keen motivation to learn English, though Saleh seems to have little opportunity in his particular neighbourhood to engage socially with English people. The informants never suggest that there is any conflict between learning English and maintaining Arabic.

While on the subject of Arabic maintenance, it is relevant to mention that there are at least three Arabic complementary schools in Sheffield, one of which is supported by the Yemeni Community Association (YCA) and has around two hundred pupils. ➡*see also Part 2: Portuguese and Chinese schools in London p97 and Part 3: Initial teacher education for community language teachers p152*. The YCA has also liaised productively with the city council to initiate the Yemeni Literacy campaign and the Yemeni Carers Project (Chatterjee 2001). It supports the Yemeni Economic and Training Centre and has helped establish a much used Yemeni Advice Centre.

Despite the high unemployment, bad housing and poor health currently experienced by Yemenis in Sheffield, there is a sense of optimism that as the younger generation progresses through the school system, with some entering higher education, employment prospects will brighten.

Barcelona and Catalonia:
Between an old paradox and a new opportunity
Silvia Carrasco, Universitat Autònoma de Barcelona

Barcelona is a leading cosmopolitan city in the western Mediterranean basin, an important artistic and economic centre and a destination for tourists from all over the world. It is also the capital city of Catalonia, one of the Autonomous Communities into which Spain is administratively divided. It was an independent kingdom in medieval times that witnessed the birth and hazardous survival of Catalan, one of the most ancient languages in Europe, which evolved from Latin more than one thousand years ago.

Ever since the formation of the Spanish state, the people of Catalonia have struggled to maintain their language against a monolingual and monocultural ideology that privileged Spanish over Catalan. Paradoxically, this struggle has led to another monolingual ideology in which other languages are seen as a threat to Catalan. Therefore, in the new context of substantial migration to Barcelona and Catalonia, there is often a resistance to developing multilingual and multicultural identities. Here I discuss the historical background to these views, and consider how the education system can take the opportunity to construct an inclusive multilingual environment that also maintains Catalan.

Historical context
By the end of the eighteenth century, the industrial revolution had already emerged in Catalonia, in contrast to the rest of Spain at the time. Immigrants

from nearby regions, both Catalan (from the Mediterranean region) and Spanish speakers, were soon followed by immigrants from all over Spain. For decades, most of them were linguistically assimilated into Catalan and became bilingual, as they were relatively few in numbers and had the same factory employment, areas of residence and cultural activities as local people.

During the nineteenth century, conflicts between Catalonia and the ruling centre of the Spanish state continued, but there was a renaissance of literature in Catalan. A romantic nationalist movement and later a modernist political and cultural movement were supported by the Catalan bourgeoisie as well as the working class. After the Spanish Civil War, however, the use of Catalan was forbidden in all spheres. The school system that had developed during the eight years of Republican government, privileging the use of Catalan as a medium of instruction, was completely dismantled.

Shortly afterwards, industrial reorganisation and the demand for labour led to new waves of migration from Spanish speaking areas of Spain to Catalonia. The Catalan language became a symbol of internal cohesion in opposition to Franco's regime and to the traditional centralism of the Spanish state, creating a positive attitude towards it among working class Spanish speaking immigrants.

When democracy was restored, regions of Spain regained autonomous rule in important areas of policy, particularly education and language. After the *Llei de Normalització Lingüística* (Act on Linguistic Normalisation) was passed, the school curriculum was taught in the endangered language (Catalan), while the dominant language (Spanish) became a curriculum subject. A language immersion programme in Catalan, inspired by the model in Quebec, was developed for the children of Spanish speaking families. However, the response to Catalan dominant schooling was not altogether positive. In spite of an increased oral and written knowledge of Catalan, people's attitudes towards the language and its social use began to change. Its previously unquestioned prestige started to weaken.

New migrations

From the mid-90s the position of Catalan was further affected by an increase in immigration from all over the world. This took place as a result of globalisation and international migration trends, together with the new political and economic position of Spain as a member state and southern border of the European Union. Whereas in Barcelona in 1995, 0.5% of school pupils were from other countries, the percentage had reached 10.5% only ten years later, in 2005. Many of the new arrivals were from Latin America, especially Ecuador, and were surprised to find that their children faced a compulsory requirement to learn Catalan for school. This constituted another unexpected problem to overcome in the hardship of migration and sometimes generated attitudes of resistance, especially in secondary schools. For other immigrants too, the requirement for Catalan seemed arbitrary since the language used in the street was mostly Spanish and children's peers at school also tended to speak Spanish to each other.

These conditions put additional pressure on Catalan as an endangered language. The new context required an imaginative response that would foster positive attitudes towards Catalan amongst an increasingly diverse younger generation. However, during the initial period of increased immigration (1995-2003), right-wing governments were in power, and there was an openly assimilationist approach to linguistic and cultural diversity. Pupils new to Catalan were seen from a deficit perspective. Rather than using the new situation as an opportunity to review ethnocentric curricular contents or outdated teaching methods, the educational system concentrated on special classes to host pupils until they acquired sufficient Catalan to be incorporated into the mainstream. Thus a research project during this period (Carrasco and Soto, 2003) revealed that although 42 languages were being spoken by school-children in Barcelona and 14% of children lived in multilingual households, schools did not positively value or build on this multilingual capital.

During the second and most recent period of immigration, there was an average of a 40% annual increase in the numbers of immigrant pupils for three consecutive school years from 2004 onwards. In 2004, a left-wing coalition took over the autonomous government and developed a new set of linguistic and educational policies called *Pla de Llengua, Interculturalitat i Cohesió Social* (Plan for Language, Intercultural Education and Social Cohesion). This plan included welcome and reception classes for all newly arrived immigrant pupils at every school, regardless of the family language, the development of a special advisory service to support teachers, an in-service teacher training programme in schools, a plan to support school leadership as a tool for community development (*Pla d'Entorn*), and the production of new materials on research findings and good practice. The policy has also fostered the organisation of extracurricular workshops for children and families in the languages of immigrant communities, beginning with Arabic, Tamazight, Chinese, Urdu and Romanian. Until these languages become part of the regular curriculum, students can claim an official certificate from the Department of Education that assesses their home language knowledge

Initiatives in multilingual schools

In spite of these important changes in perspectives and policies in recent years, cultural and linguistic hierarchies still persist in large sectors of education and there is insufficient support for pupils to develop multiple identities within school. However, a further stage of the Barcelona research project mentioned above, conducted in 2002-2005 in Ciutat Vella, the heart of the old city in Barcelona where more than 40% of parents of schoolchildren were immigrants, revealed some good practice in schools. For example, one secondary school that successfully promotes academic achievement has created a website in which students present their multicultural backgrounds, while you can also learn their languages online (www.ravalnet.org/iestarradell/lm/). A primary school has developed an initiative looking at past and present immigration to the area through the lives of children in different historical periods in the same neighbourhood, linking children's experiences with world events.

These schools have found that an environment which values children's multilingual identities leads to a positive attitude towards Catalan and an understanding of what the language means for local people. This promotes the learning of Catalan. The school thus becomes a space where children and young people share their experiences, and Catalan becomes a shared language. As a result, moves to displace the multiethnic population and gentrify the area in Ciutat Vella have been contested by youth and neighbourhood organisations working together through Catalan to promote positive images of different ethnic groups.

2. Website where pupils teach their languages, Miquel Tarradell School, Barcelona.

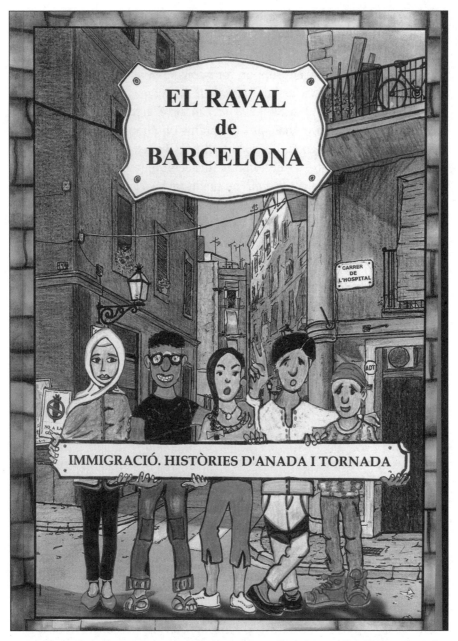

3. Front cover of book by young people telling their stories of migration to the neighbourhood of Raval in Ciutat Vella, Barcelona.

Barcelona's challenge, therefore, is to combine the struggle against the loss of the Catalan language with the development of multilingual skills and multicultural identities, to create an environment in which people can feel part of a world city in an era of transnational communication.

Whilst new migrations offer an opportunity to do this, it is important to remember the words of Carme Junyent, the renowned Catalan specialist in endangered languages: 'Hope will only exist if we can recognise the contributions that these multifarious ways of seeing the world make. If there is recognition, there will be reciprocity' (Junyent, 2004:174).

Connections in cyberspace: Implications for Tamil diasporic communities
Siva Pillai and Jim Anderson, Goldsmiths, University of London

The internet is fast becoming a major medium for the consolidation, strengthening and definition of collective identities, especially in the absence of a firm territorial and institutional base (Erikson, 2006)

In 1998 the website 'tamilnation.org' was launched by Nadesan Satyendra to nurture the 'growing togetherness' of more than 70 million Tamil people living in over 50 countries across the world, including an estimated 300,000 in the UK, 60,000 in France, 50,000 in Germany, 40,000 in Switzerland, 25,000 in Italy, 20,000 in the Netherlands, 10,000 in Norway, 7,000 in Denmark and 2,000 in Sweden (Sivasupramaniam, 2004). Against the background of a 25 year-old civil war and the struggle to create an independent *Tamil Eelam* in the north and east of Sri Lanka, the site proclaims the existence of a transnational Tamil state based on commitment to a shared history, language and culture and realised through the power of digital technology.

Here we explore the significance of the rapid technological advances that have taken place in the past fifteen years for the Tamil diasporic community, in particular for those living in the UK. We focus on how these developments are affecting people at three levels: personal, community and educational.

Personal
Digital communications have played a major role in overcoming the barriers of distance and time, and the implications of this for people living outside their homeland have been very significant. Forty years ago, maintaining contact with family and friends in Sri Lanka was far from easy. Letters took seven

days to arrive. Phone calls were expensive and connections slow and un-reliable. There was no access to Tamil television programmes. Newspapers and magazines sent from Sri Lanka were out of date by the time they reached the UK. It was hard not to feel isolated.

Within a few decades the situation has changed dramatically. Telecommuni-cations are cheaper and more efficient. Tamil radio and television channels are easily available. Most significantly, the internet provides the means for instant access to websites created by Tamils living not just in India and Sri Lanka, but right across the world. Moreover, as the technology has advanced it has become possible to read online versions of newspapers and magazines, and even to download music and films. Through email, chat rooms, discus-sion groups, smart groups, internet telephony networks such as Skype, and most recently through blogs, opportunities have been created for links with family and friends across the globe to be maintained and for important family events to be shared and celebrated. For the 'net generation' (Tapscott, 1998) in particular, the new technology has instilled a sense of confidence through participation in a global youth culture expressed in fashion, music and film.

English tends to dominate as a mode of communication between more highly educated Tamils, particularly amongst second and third generation immigrants, and this is reflected in communication on the internet. Whilst this trend may be worrying in relation to the maintenance of Tamil language and culture, it is important to bear several points in mind. Firstly, there is a technical issue. Until a Tamil Unicode font was introduced in the Microsoft operating system, downloading the software required to view Tamil script was a laborious process. Secondly, English is an official language in India and widely spoken throughout south Asia as well as having high status as an inter-national lingua franca. Thus use of English enables a wider audience to be reached. However, there is now a trend towards greater use of indigenous lan-guages on websites, which are increasingly bilingual or multilingual.

However, not everyone has been in a position to take advantage of these new opportunities. In Sri Lanka and in the Indian state of Tamil Nadu, internet connection is still only available in the large cities. For Tamils living in other parts of the world, the extent to which it is possible to join the virtual com-munity depends on levels of access to networked computers.

Community

The flexibility of the internet means that it not only encourages a sense of global connectedness, but also supports community networking and support at the local level. A good example is the LondonTamilan site which claims to be 'the biggest and most popular online community and social/professional networking hub for Tamilan in the United Kingdom'. The site is also intended for wider national and international audiences and seeks 'to unite all Tamilan around the globe'. This multi-level approach is reflected in the news and in the business and investment sections which cover Tamil activities at local, national and international levels.

At local level, the site provides links to various religious and welfare organisations as well as information and photo galleries on cultural and sporting events of interest to the London-based community. These include the Hindu Chariot Festival, the Tamil School Sport Festival, the Tamil Youth Organisation Western Kuthu (drama) and Women's Day. In this way the site encourages a sense of community solidarity as well as offering a means of celebrating cultural heritage. It also means that Tamil communities in other parts of the UK or elsewhere can keep in touch with and possibly gain inspiration from what's going on in London.

A site aimed particularly at Tamil youth is 'londontamilgirlsboys'. The site features material related to popular Indian and Sri Lankan films and music, but its main purpose is clearly to encourage young Tamils to socialise with each other in its chatroom and there is a facility for members to post photos of themselves.

In addition to the growing number of websites, the importance of local Tamil TV and radio stations should also be noted. Sun TV UK Ltd, Deepam TV and CITV broadcast 24 hours a day throughout Europe and the Middle East and a majority of Tamil families subscribe to these. The channels provide local as well as European and global news from a Tamil perspective. Films and soap operas feature prominently and there is a range of programmes aimed at children, including educational programmes to support them in learning both Tamil and English. There are also several UK based Tamil radio stations, the most well-known of which are Sunrise Radio and the International Broadcasting Corporation (IBC) – Tamil. These stations, as well as providing general news and entertainment, encourage lively debate on issues affecting the local Tamil community.

Educational

Whilst Tamils have been successful in building new lives for themselves and their families in countries across the world, there has been growing concern that young Tamils, in particular, may be losing touch with their linguistic and cultural roots. The internet has a major role to play in providing a solution to this problem, not least because many expatriate Tamils are computer professionals at the forefront of their field. The Tamil Virtual University (TVU), set up in 1999 by the government of Tamil Nadu and freely accessible, offers certificated courses at three levels as well as a BA programme in Tamil. Some interactive language learning material aimed at primary age children is also provided. In his report to the TVU, Harrigan (1999) stresses the importance of employing appropriate pedagogical models for teaching Tamil to diaspora Tamils and non-Tamils, pointing out that the majority want to acquire modern spoken and written Tamil rather than ancient classical or literary varieties of Tamil and that the emphasis should be on practical communication.

Of the many websites dedicated to teaching Tamil, the most comprehensive and highly regarded have been developed at the University of Pennsylvania. Launched in 1997, the Web Assisted Learning and Teaching of Tamil (WALTT) project, led by Prof. Harold F. Schiffman and Dr. Vasu Renganathan, is a structured bank of text-based, audio and video material, intended primarily to support courses in Tamil language at the university for students with limited or no knowledge of the language. In 2004 this work was extended through the creation of a linked site, Tamil Language in Context, funded by the University of Chicago South Asia Language Resource Center with the aim of creating a comprehensive online Tamil textbook, supported with video clips and incorporating a high level of interactivity. These projects have been based on a second language learning pedagogy aimed at enabling students to gain basic communicative competence in the language. They have made a significant impact both in the United States and beyond because they make the process of learning the language meaningful and enjoyable, so providing a model for others to follow.

Another important resource is the Tamil Electronic Library, created in 1995 by Dr. K.Kalyanasundaram of the Swiss Federal Institute of Technology at Lausanne, Switzerland. The library contains a range of resources on Tamil language, literature, history and culture, including electronic texts of literary classics.

The *Curriculum Guide for Tamil* (Pillai and Nithiya, 2007) is a new resource for the teaching of Tamil to children, developed at Goldsmiths College and linked to the Asset Languages qualifications for Tamil which were recently introduced as part of the UK's National Languages Strategy. The *Guide* has been designed primarily to support the work of Tamil teachers working in

4. Teaching material from Tamil website by Pollachi Nasan: each letter lights up as the sound is heard.

மரம் (Tree)

சக்கரம்
(wheel)

over 40 Tamil community schools across the UK and to support recognition of children's achievement in the language. It is based on an up-to-date communicative approach to language teaching in which use of information and communications technology has a key role. Resources to support teachers in delivering activities proposed in the *Guide*, including Powerpoint files and material for use with the interactive whiteboard, are provided on the Goldsmiths community-gold website to which there is free access.

A further bank of resources related to the *Guide*, but intended for a wider audience, is being developed through partnership with Pollachi Nasan, an educational advisor for Tamil language in South India, and can be viewed on his website. These up-to-date interactive resources, which use images, animation and sound and video clips, are intended for use both in the classroom and at home. In creating the *Guide*, there has also been valuable collaboration with Tamil colleagues in France, Germany, Switzerland and Norway, facililitated by fast communication and easy transfer of documents over the internet. In future it is hoped to develop internet-based partnerships with schools in Sri Lanka, India and elsewhere through international linking schemes.

Conclusion

For those who have access to it, the internet and other technological advances contribute significantly to enabling Tamils, in whatever country they might be residing, to feel part of a living Tamil culture. Within this virtual space, bilingual and bicultural identities can be shaped and given expression, which leads to complex debates on whether and how western perspectives can be integrated with more traditional values. Overall, however, connections in cyberspace have made it possible for people to shift between different spheres of their lives, balancing various social, cultural, religious and moral perspectives, holding onto the past whilst embracing the future and in the process developing syncretic identities and a sense of themselves as citizens of the world.

2

Constructing identity through creativity and narrative

This chapter describes identity construction in groups and at a personal level, in three creative projects: bilingual theatre written by young people of Bosnian heritage in London, carnival in South London schools, and digital photography in Cyprus. The projects reflect some of the choices available to different groups and individuals of how to represent their identities as narratives through social and aesthetic action, using music, dance, drama and visual media. Each account shows how young people seize the opportunity to develop responses to issues within their own communities via both individual and collaborative creative expression. In so doing, they develop outcomes with resonances for society as a whole.

Bilingual Theatre
Dina Mehmedbegovic, Institute of Education, London

Why bilingual theatre?

Bilingual theatre is an attempt to project on stage the experience of living in two languages. My own visual representation of the inner world of a bilingual is a lively spa that feeds on and produces jets of vocabulary and structures in two different languages. These constantly cascade over each other and into each other. Their existence is intertwined and inseparable. This lively and complex world of bilinguality is invisible and inaudible in most mainstream settings where bilinguals discipline themselves to produce the output in one language only, the dominant language of their environment. Bilinguality will only find its external embodiment when bilinguals communicate with bilinguals who have the same languages in common. In such a setting many bilinguals will comfortably slip into what comes naturally: code mixing and code switching. The initiative to write and stage a play in two languages was driven by the idea of allowing the inner world of bilinguality to spill out, pour onto the stage and claim legitimate life through a shared, public, creative exploration.

The project described here was allocated funding by London Arts Board in 1998. The aim was to work with a group of young people who were bilingual in Bosnian and English to produce a play in those two languages, to be shown during the Young Writers Festival in the year 2000 at the Royal Court Theatre in London, a theatre known for presenting new drama.

Project structure

In November 1999, workshops to develop mutual trust and communication began with a group of 30 bilinguals aged 14 to19. All had left their home country because of the war in former Yugoslavia. As soon as it became obvious that the project was going to be a significant time commitment – almost all weekends over a period of the following ten months – the number of young people willing to sign up was down to five.

Once the core group was established, the workshops became structured writing sessions with the focus on individual and shared writing. A demanding pace was set through providing instant feedback from the group and the director. As our thematic starting point we took the theme of 'Journeys'. Every participant had an interesting story to tell, either based on their own experience or the experience of somebody close to them. The play gradually grew into a mosaic of different journeys: a boy leaving his home in Sarajevo, saying goodbye to his best friend and his new bicycle; a sister going back to Bosnia looking for her brother who was lost in the midst of war; a father and son on a journey of transformed identities; a young man going back to Sarajevo to the sadness of a sudden loss of childhood; young people from different walks of life on an ordinary train journey in England.

The long-standing question of what we were going to call the play was resolved when, many months into the writing, one of the young people received notification of his right to become a British citizen. With the joy of finding his sense of belonging formally acknowledged and with the thrill of being able to travel again, he phoned the director the same day and said, '*Naturalised!!* Let's call it *Naturalised!*'

Naturalised was performed for five nights at the Royal Court in November 2000. Due to its success it was offered a further three nights at the Half Moon Theatre in East London. Who attended? Many members of the participants' families, friends, teachers, monolinguals and bilinguals, the Bosnian ambassador at the time – all eight nights were sold out. Everybody came out full of praise for *Naturalised*.

Creating bilingually

The project took over the premises of the Royal Court Young People's Theatre on Saturdays and Sundays from the end of 1999 to September 2000. The young writers regularly occupied a random collection of second-hand armchairs dotted around the spacious premises adjacent to the main building, as they worked on the scenes of *Naturalised*. Once the set time for writing was up, the dotted armchairs would gather into a circle for a period of sharing and discussing. What contributed to the dynamics of those encounters was that the director was British and unfamiliar with all things Bosnian. Therefore, for the young people in the group, there was a real need and motive to describe and define relevant aspects of their background and experience.

Throughout the project, participants were encouraged to communicate and express themselves in their first language as well as in English. It was noticed that most of the pair work would happen in Bosnian. However, the independent writing which was produced with the aim of obtaining feedback from the English-speaking director was produced in English. Only one participant from Croatia, who was new to English at the time, had written mostly in Croatian.

Soon it became clear that the use of both languages – which came naturally in oral expression within the group – was not easily transferable into the written form. Reflecting back on this, one possible explanation is that the young people's previous experience of writing was in a mainstream school, where the expectation was that only one language would be used. So, asking them suddenly to write bilingually was alien and confusing, because they had learnt to cut off this aspect of their bilinguality at the point of writing. They did not know how to begin using two languages in their scenes, unless it was as a direct translation. Using translation was not what we were aiming for, because translation is a function of bilinguality that is used to bridge two separate languages. In many ways it is the opposite of how bilinguals usually express their inner worlds.

We tried exercises: you have two minutes; write anything that comes to you. Still the inhibitions held their creativity in a paralysing grip. Three months later, many scenes were written – but monolingually. They explored the experiences of overcoming language barriers, trying to integrate into the new environment, first language maintenance issues, and negotiating different cultures. But the bilingual nature of the experiences remained on the content level only.

The breakthrough happened with the scene *Zatrlić not Smith*, the first part of which is reproduced at the end of the chapter. This became one of the central scenes of the play. It is – like all the other scenes – based on a true story. It is about a father going down an emotional spiral triggered by the initiative of his 8-year-old son who wanted to replace an unpronounceable Bosnian surname with Smith. The boy wants to avoid being laughed at, while the father feels betrayed, hurt, alienated and a failure on the personal and professional level. The moment of truth and reconciliation is brought on by the poem written by the boy:

> **In the heart in the body in the land**
> *My life*
> *In the land on this planet in space*
> *My home*
> *By the tree in the playground in school*
> *My friend*
> *In my father in my mother in me*
> *My name*
> (From *Naturalised*)

The project participant who wrote this scene started using Bosnian to mark the most emotional moments of the father's anger, and the boy's tearful begging for mercy. This met with the approval of the whole group, because everybody was able to identify with the authenticity of slipping into their first language at highly emotional times. From then on the bilingual dimension of the play started growing in different directions. Some participants were using their first language in a variety of ways: to create trust between characters, or to add authenticity to a casual conversation between two bilinguals. Some participants started producing bilingual scenes just for the sake of experimenting with bilingual expression.

The play contains several scenes that are de-contextualised vignettes of conversations in a shop or a lift using not only Bosnian and English, but the eastern and western dialects of Bosnian to suggest cultural and political conflicts amongst the population of the same home country. The feeling was that our bilingual young people had been set free. Their written products were finally reflecting their oral bilingual communication, thinking processes and inner dialogue. The following scene takes place in a coffee shop where Bosnians of different backgrounds (Bosnian and Serbian) meet. The phrases used are common to the Bosnian and Serbian languages. However, the speakers cannot agree on what constitutes 'our language' or 'our country':

A: *Dobar dan. Zdravo.*
B: Good afternoon.
A: *Do-bar dan??*
B: Good af-ter-noon???
A: Why do you insist on this rubbish?
B: Oh, don't make me start.
A: *Dobro onda, imaš li kafe?*
B: We are out of coffee.
A: *Jel', mi se onda ne* understand *baš* best.
B: *Oh ne, mi se* understand *vrlo* good.
A: *Pa je'l ti to tamo kafa stoji il' me praviš ludim??*
B: No, that's not coffee over there. You'll find that's just empty space.
A: Hey, we were friends. Remember ... Same city, same country.
B: Same city, different country.
A: Same country.
B: Different country.
A: Our country.
B: Our country.
A: Our country for god's sake, same language.
B: I recall a different language.
A: Our language.
B: Yes, perhaps our language, but different language.
A: *Znači da me razumiješ?* Yes?
B: I don't understand you. Leave. Please. Now.
A: *Al' neću se vraćat' da znaš.*
B: Then don't come back. Go back to your country.

All the scenes are written with the intention of communicating the content without translating. Obviously, the stage version of the text provides visual clues as well, which additionally help the audience to understand.

Bilingual theatre as a response to wider educational and social issues

Even though all the participants were new to theatre and playwriting, they showed great learning potential and a range of transferable skills. In their evaluation forms they indicated that working on this project was a truly novel and educational experience.

The stage of the project that created the highest level of interest and enthusiasm was working in rehearsals with the director, actors, sound engineer and costume designer. The participants had an opportunity to take an active part in the process of transforming their text into a theatre performance. Insights and guidance provided by professionals with different expertise helped them add new qualities to their scenes. By watching the professional actors shape the text on stage the participants learnt about multi-layered ways of communicating. This led to many adjustments of the text and to improved energy in the play.

Working with professionals was the key principle of this project. It enhanced the creativity and developed the skills of young people at an extraordinary rate. It made the final product look polished, professional and sophisticated.

In terms of multilingual identities, bilingual theatre for me was a creative response to observing children rejecting their first language for the kinds of reasons which are common to many young bilinguals growing up in Britain's monolingualising society. It was an attempt to counterbalance the factors which contribute to the low value of first languages in the mainstream society and their consequent loss.

Excerpt from Naturalised Scene 6: Zatrlić not Smith

Teacher (Calling register) David Green (waits for response), Simon Hunter, Lisa Metcalf, Emma Davis, Stephen Watson, Emily Jones, Bojan Zat ... Zatrul ... I'm sorry Bojan ...

Lights up slowly revealing a modest household. There is a huge blackboard in the middle of the room. A small boy Bojan, aged 8, is writing on the board. There are a lot of books piled up on the table: Marx, Nietzsche, Plato, Mill.

The boy eventually starts repeatedly writing 'Zatrlić' on the board, he speeds up writing it then slows down, then speeds up again. Boy's father gets up from the armchair, starts pacing up and down.

Bojan: *Tata, ja ne mogu vise ...*

Father: *Ćuti!!*

Bojan: Please dad ...

Father: *Ćuti!! 300 puta rekao sam.* I said 300 times!!!! You ungrateful little ...

Bojan: But it's not like that, I mean, I just didn't want ...

Father: *Ćuti!!!* Insult upon insult! Who do you think you are? You are 8 years old and you insult your own flesh and blood ...

Bojan continues writing 'Zatrlić'. He suddenly writes 'Smith'. His father sees it. He starts towards the son. The son freezes in fear. They stare at each other.

With special thanks to the young writers: Martina Grgečić, Mirna Jančić, Omar Smailbegović, Ismar Uzeirović and Miroslav Vranić; Steve Gilroy, Rufus Norris and everybody at The Royal Court Young People's Theatre.

Children learning to use the creative languages of carnival

Celia Burgess-Macey, Goldsmiths, University of London

Why is there a chapter on carnival in a book about multilingual communities? For many families within the UK's diasporic communities, carnival is an important medium of expression. The languages of carnival are music, dance, drama and masquerade.

The history of Notting Hill carnival is inextricably linked with the struggle for survival and recognition of the African Caribbean black community. Its central cultural and aesthetic practices replicate those of Caribbean carnivals, which in themselves are a syncretic mix of cultural influences from Africa, Europe, Asia and the Americas. There has been a long history of negative media representation which meant it was a challenge to get carnival taken seriously within schools. However the recognition of carnival arts by national arts funding bodies and education authorities has opened up a space within which carnival can develop at schools.

To discuss children's learning of carnival languages, I have drawn on data from three projects: a teacher exchange project in two primary schools in London and in Trinidad (2001); a school linking project between three primary schools in South London and two in Trinidad (2003); and the HEARTS project 'Carnival and Performing Arts in Education' at Goldsmiths, involving seven primary schools (2005-6). Evidence will be mainly drawn from schools in the UK. The following are key themes from all projects.

Carnival was a supportive context for developing children's creativity

Craft (2005) discusses how creativity is linked to 'possibility thinking' and needs to tap into children's passions and capabilities. Children designed costumes, researched their theme, envisioned what the costume might look like and what it might feel like to wear it, and communicated their design to others. This involves emotional as well as intellectual work. Only the desire to be inside the costume can explain the attention even very young children were able to give to this. Themes included the abstract and the familiar: Earth, Air, Fire and Water, Saving the Environment, The Slave Trade Abolition Act, Myths and Legends and well loved stories.

> The children were Woodland Fairies, so the nursery nurse got lots of leaf shapes and patterns and coloured fabric and different coloured netting and they chose what

46

colours and fabrics they wanted and stuck it on their design board and that was how they planned for their costume. [Teacher]

Each child drew a picture of their Dragon costume and then I wrote down what the child had told me about it like it has to have a spiky tail or it has to breathe fire so those were the elements that they had to include when they were building the costume. [Teacher]

The link between culture and creativity (DfEE, 1999) is apparent in the collaborative cultural practices of carnival. There is a relationship between the individual and the group that is essential to dance, construction of masquerade and music making, and this supported individual children in finding their own creative spark. They were also supported by working with artist practitioners from within carnival culture.

I was with a group of about five kids ... and I started to hit this beat on the floor which of course comes from a physical dynamic. And we started what was almost like a jazz riff. And these kids were composing and if we had stayed there we would have ended up composing a new piece of work ... [Greta Mendez, dancer]

Children exploited the meaning making potential of carnival through play

Representing ideas and feelings visually is central to the development of symbolic and abstract thinking (DfES, 2007a). For young children carnival activities reinforced the role of play in learning. Designing and making as well as the dance and performances of masquerade involved dramatising and role play.

... after we discussed the story, they decided what animal they wanted to be and I said 'How do you want your jaguar to be? Will it be a friendly jaguar or will it be a fierce jaguar?' and so on. Lots of them wanted their jaguar to be scary. K said he wanted his jaguar to be a very powerful jaguar ... and that is a great feeling to be something more powerful and scary ... I was surprised that in the end only three girls wanted to be butterflies. They were just as keen on being jaguars with sharp teeth and sharp claws as the boys were ... it actually gave the girls an opportunity to explore that more powerful side. [Teacher]

Children explored meaning through Bruner's three modes: enactive (using movement), iconic (using images created by themselves) and symbolic (using symbols from the culture) (Bruner, 1982). They used the multimodal communication that is familiar from popular culture.

Because the guys see them on television whether it is rapping or street talk or calypso or reggae. Some of the symbols and body language I use it as positiveness and there you find the guys get more involved, what I try to do is to mix in the modern-day thing, the street gestures. [Jackie Guy, dancer]

This process was particularly apparent in 'playing mas' (putting on your mask or costume and moving with it, taking part in the masquerade).

If you really want to create your mas it has to come from inside. You get the influences from outside but what are the rhythms what are the pulses which are unique to them ... what I found so refreshing, that you could get people of the age of 4, 5 and 6 to that level of focus. That focus comes from the tips of their toes. It is in every fibre. [Greta Mendez, dancer]

Working with artists, one another and parents on carnival activities was a significant scaffold for children's learning

For some children and teachers, carnival discourse had been learnt in the context of family and community where children had access to 'funds of knowledge', the term used by Moll *et al* to describe the cultural resources built up in particular communities (Moll *et al*, 1992).

My experience as a child was that once you have got this costume on it is not so important how fantastically well it has been made, it is just the fact of transforming and becoming something else that is fantastic. [Teacher]

Carnival artists drew teachers' attention to this potential resource for learning so children could use the tools of their culture in interaction with significant others through 'guided participation' (Rogoff, 1990). Children were thus able to collaborate in new ways:

It's taken quite a long time for some children to work cooperatively. And this project has really enhanced those skills. It was working towards a very clear goal that helped. I think they knew the carnival was going to be a special and important day. It's just that whole idea of celebrating together ... most of the children are quite interested in the idea of being part of a big group, in that sort of identity. [Teacher]

I felt like I came from a real band and we made up our Calypso like a real team. We made up our own music and I really enjoyed it. [Child]

Parents were also more willing to be involved, by working creatively with others from different cultural backgrounds and with their own children.

➡ *see also Part 2: Parent-teacher partnerships p89.*

➡ *see also Part 2: Parent-teacher partnerships p89.*

The parents' literacy group designed and made the carnival banner ... they came up with the ideas for the banner themselves. We were able to discuss the fact that carnival is not just about celebrating but that it has also got other levels of meaning to it ...They talked about their own festivals. One of the mothers who is a Shiite

Muslim talked about one of the big festivals around the death of the Prophet Mohammed when they all come out in the streets. [Teacher]

You will notice a lot of the wings have intricate patterns in glitter where the parents have helped the children. As they did it they were talking to their children and so when the child said it needs to have fire, the parents put that in, pockets of fire coming out of it. [Teacher]

Encounters with carnival artists supported the exploration of identities in these multicultural classrooms

Few of the children who participated in my research in London had had personal experience of the Notting Hill carnival. Most had never encountered carnival as an aspect of black history or popular culture. Artists made this link for them, and the children responded positively with a new confidence in their identities and the creative work they were able to produce.

Particularly the boys seemed ignorant of the pride they can have in their own black history and I started with a song, 'What is black music?' It questions how long black musicians have influenced music and I go back to Hadrian, when the Romans were here building the wall and he had seven black trumpeters playing for him ... to tell them 'no you have this history of greatness.' And the boys quite visibly perked up, so when the time came to write their calypsos they said 'Oh yes we will write this'. [Alexander D Great, calypsonian]

... children recognised her voice as something from home, her voice was familiar to them, so that was a positive thing ... I think they were surprised by her high expectations. [Teacher discussing workshop with Nadella Benjamin, masquerade designer]

Carnival supported children's access to the curriculum and was an inclusive learning experience

Carnival's different art forms offered children multi-modal learning experiences which enabled everyone to participate.

When you look at their body language you can see the sense of achievement. It's about self-confidence ... when you try the movement and the mas you might have a shy child and at the end of the session this person come alive. [Jackie Guy, dancer]

A teacher described what happened to a child with attention and communication issues.

She was just threading tiny buttons onto tiny laces, all the most intricate tiniest things she has been fantastic at and she has made no fuss ... I think it was the fact that she was making it for herself. Making it for her own body. Making it for herself to wear. [Teacher]

There are also inclusion issues for some African Caribbean children in schools who experience marginalisation of their forms and styles of communication, and their visual, musical and literary cultures (Callender, 1997). It has been argued that this is a causal factor in the under-achievement of African Caribbean children, especially boys (Gillborn and Gipps, 1996). Boykin (1994) suggests that teachers need to incorporate 'Afro cultural ethos' into the culture of the classroom and to value movement and musical expression, group identity, expressive individualism and oral communication – all exemplified in carnival activities.

> I saw a boy who we normally have a lot of behaviour issues with. He was holding hands with a little girl in the class and they were twirling each other around and doing all these lovely dance moves and normally he would only pretend to be a Power Ranger. It has highlighted their skills. [Teacher]

> We were all singing and enjoying ourselves and dancing and it felt like I should go to Trinidad and experience it myself ... and it shows how much fun you can have and it makes me feel like I want to go back to the Caribbean and share my experience. [Child]

Conclusion

Carnival arts activities were valued by both teachers and children. All children must be able to use the resources of history, language and culture in defining themselves. Work on the projects confirmed that carnival arts can develop children's individuality and enhance their sense of belonging, while they are learning to be self-reliant, inventive, creative and imaginative.

The official curriculum in schools has allowed insufficient space for children to draw on their 'funds of knowledge' and has frequently failed to recognise the considerable knowledge and skills of adults in their communities. As teachers and teacher educators we need to embrace notions of diversity and find ways of representing ourselves with many voices, many languages. Carnival is one of those languages.

The way we are: Multilingual photographic journeys for children in Cyprus

Aydin Mehmet Ali

This project brought digital photography to a village in North Cyprus, enabling Cypriotgreek and Cypriotturkish children to explore their shared lives and spaces. The findings demonstrate that although there are great difficulties in running multicultural, multilingual projects in militarised and divided societies, artists can play a key role in defusing racial and ethnic tensions through creative work, especially amongst marginalised communities.

The socio-political background

The historical and political conditions that gave rise to the divided state of Cyprus are complex and contested. Despite initiatives from the UN and EU alongside bilateral negotiations between Turkey and Greece, North and South Cyprus currently remain separated, and people may even lack knowledge of the map of the 'other side'. This story takes place in the village of Ayia Triada (its original Cypriotgreek name) or Sipahi (as it was named after the 1974 invasion as part of Turkification), situated on a mountainside in the remote Karpaz peninsula in North Cyprus.

While this was a thriving village before 1974, with its own bank, large school, olive mill and historical tenth century ruin attracting tourists, soon after the invasion most Cypriotgreek villagers went to the south as refugees. Settlers then came from the Black Sea area of Turkey. Meanwhile, Cypriotturkish refugees from the south arrived in the neighbouring larger village of Yialoussa/ Yeni Erenkoy.

Contact with people from other countries or even from outside the village is very limited, and the area is heavily militarised. Despite this, there are good relationships between the Cypriotgreek and Black Sea settler families in the village. The latter arrived with the ability to speak an ancient form of Greek due to the history of the Black Sea area, and could therefore try to communicate with the Cypriotgreek population. The ruling elite sees the two groups as enemy communities but in fact they share everyday life and village spaces.

The village has the rare benefit of two functioning churches with permission to ring their bells! A new mosque has been built as part of the attempts at Islamisation, despite many in the village being secular. The village is neglected and isolated, and suffers serious socio-economic and educational disadvantages, but its multicultural, multilingual and multifaith composition is rare in North Cyprus. These factors made it an important location for our photographic project.

The project's aims

We wanted to give young people the opportunity to tell their own stories about life in the village, using photography to construct their own images. The project involved artists from the UK who already had experience of using the arts to defuse tensions in Cypriot settings in London. By bringing the latest ICT equipment to the village, we could introduce these disadvantaged young people and their families to high quality art work and help them develop new skills. We planned to organise photography workshops and then work with the villagers to produce a photographic exhibition to be held first in their village and at a later stage in Nicosia, London, Turkey and Greece. The project would highlight the existing positive relations between people of different languages and faiths in this village, raising the visibility of a community long neglected and ignored by the Cypriot mainstream.

Making a start

Access to new technologies hardly existed in the village before the arrival of the project team. Only one person had a computer and it did not work, and nobody had a digital camera. The project workers brought digital cameras and laptops for children and families to use. At first, some adults were suspicious, asking if we were there to win votes for the coming election, whether we were going to use the photographs for propaganda purposes and whether we were going to show them on the 'other' side. However, others were interested in our equipment as they had only seen photos of such items in magazines, and now they could touch them. After a while we began taking photos of them, with their permission. The photos were instantly visible on a laptop computer screen, giving a sense of immediacy. By the time the villagers were asked to take photos of each other they were pulling faces, making fun of each other and bursting into laughter when they looked at the photos on the computer screens. They began to offer criticisms of the shots, asking how they could be improved. Photography is an amazing tool that engages people on many levels.

The only base available for the project was a derelict schoolhouse. The key was found and cleaning began, with everyone joining in. The building was slowly transformed into a space for learning by covering the broken tables with large white sheets, setting up the laptops, and arranging plastic chairs. At the same time the young people were being shown how to use the cameras and video equipment and encouraged to take photos and film each other during the cleaning and setting up. The project had begun ...

At lunchtime men began to arrive, some of whom were fathers or grand-fathers. At one stage over fifteen men were looking at the morning's photos on the computer screen. This became a daily routine; they would come at lunch-time to comment on photos taken the previous day or that morning. By the afternoon, as schools are half-day, we had twenty children of all ages who had rushed to the deserted school building, having returned from their school in the neighbouring village of Yialoussa/Yeni Erenkoy.

As there were not have enough cameras and we did not want to turn anyone away, teams of two or three children were established to go out together and take pictures. They were free to photograph anything they wanted in the village. They kept asking what else they could photograph, and suggestions were offered such as families and friends, favourite places and a sequence creating a story. The project leaders did not accompany the children, which gave them more freedom of choice and expression. In the event the children took some stunning photographs, which were stored in their folders, and individual files were set up for each child with their portraits.

Some children would come for about an hour and then disappear and come back again: they were working children and had to attend to fields, water trees and vegetable patches, harvest produce, tend to chickens, goats and cows, milk them, fetch water, clean the house, help make yogurt and cheese, and move the hives. Some of these activities are captured in their photographs.

One day three men from the village sat in the learning room with us. They were minders who had been ordered to report on our activities. At the end of the day one commented on what a great project it was and asked if he could help. The following day he came with a pot of black paint and brush to paint the graying blackboard as I had told him it would make an excellent back-ground for the children's photos at the exhibition.

An exhibition against the odds

Leaflets about the coming exhibition were copied in nearby Yialoussa/Yeni Erenkoy village where the mayor had made his office available in support. The headteacher of the primary school invited the artists to distribute the leaflets in all the classrooms and talk about the project. Children from Ayia Triada/Sipahi proudly jumped up saying, 'Our project, our project!' They were no longer the poor nobodies from the village no one went to; the international artists from London had chosen them. Changes were occurring in the dynamics of exclusion, marginalisation, identity and the 'other'.

However, we then received a threatening visit from two undercover police officers from a village further afield. Determined to mount the exhibition, we continued working and consulted lawyers who confirmed there was no legal basis to stop the project. The intimidation came to the attention of the national media. As project director I was interviewed on the radio and in the press, where I called on government ministries to make announcements if they had ordered the closure of the project. No announcement was made. Meanwhile, a number of villagers continued to support us in any way they could. One artist questioned by the police was protected from then on by a group of young people who became his constant companions.

Finally we were ready to set up the exhibition. Seeing all the excited children waiting at the old schoolhouse vindicated our decision to continue with the project despite threats and harassment. With amazing zeal, the children converted their workroom into an exhibition space; mops, buckets, brooms and rags were commandeered from homes, floors and walls washed, entrance and garden cleaned up. Some children raided mothers' cupboards and brought beautifully embroidered tablecloths to cover the broken, tatty tables. Others raided the village gardens and brought bunches of roses to put in plastic water bottles on the tables. A father brought extension leads and helped set up the laptops. These were used to show all 600 of the children's photos on a loop system which became one of the fascinating attractions. Whilst helping to put up the mounted panels of photographs, children became excited at the way their pictures looked so different and important.

Mothers began to arrive, saying it was time for the exhibition to open. Seeing that help was needed, they began to join in with hanging the work under guidance. More and more people began to arrive, including grandfathers and grandmothers, some leaning on their walking sticks; the village slowly began to descend on the old schoolhouse. People from other villages and from the closest village Yialoussa/Yeni Erenkoy came, saying they'd never been to the village before. Schoolteachers came, and the Deputy Head of the primary school arrived with his video camera, expressing surprise at the level of professionalism of the exhibition and work.

Some people were surprised to see shots they had taken or they were in, as they had thought these 'match-box' things were just toys not real cameras. The imam of the village laughed at the photos of his cow and of him caught snoozing on the couch.

A grandmother was so taken by a photograph of her grandchildren that she took the panel off the wall and went to show it to her daughter saying with affection, 'Oooh look at my twins!'; a salutary reminder that some people do not have the concept of 'an exhibition'. Children waited with expectation to see if we would intervene or tell her off for spoiling the exhibition. Instead, we took a photo of her while her grandson put the panel back and she smiled at us.

After a little while a police officer arrived in civilian clothes and apologetically informed me that he had orders to shut the exhibition down. I pointed out that unless he could show me a written order stating which section of which law I was contravening, I did not have to oblige. He agreed with relief and smiled. He was invited to look at the children's exhibition and spent some time talking to children and parents. When he came out he could no longer contain his exasperation, 'We should be encouraging more of these projects not trying to shut them down! Our children need these projects and we need people like you. Next time please come and do this project in my village, our doors are open to you and your team!'

However, we then received orders from one of the *mukhtars* (village leaders) to close the exhibition, threatening to call the military if we refused. With great reluctance, we had to comply to prevent any violence. Breaking the news to the children was very hard. I became upset, especially when they surrounded me asking 'Why? Why? Why?' and pleading to continue. After the initial anger and deep resentment some of the older ones wanted to know more. Once they were told about the circumstances that led to the decision, their thoughtful and mature reaction was sobering.

After we had presented the exhibition panels to the children on the steps of the schoolhouse, they rushed out of the gates and lined up along the front wall of the school from one end to the other, holding up their photographs. This shot was on the front page of the highest circulation newspaper, Kibris, a few days later with a detailed report on the project and its story.

Leaving the village was very moving. Children hung on our arms pleading with us not to leave, kissing and hugging us. Parents told us, some defiantly, that their doors were always open to us, anytime, any day, just to turn up and to come back soon. As we left in the car, the children ran after us, waving and holding the exhibition panels of photographs high up in full view of the two plainclothes police officers hiding behind the church.

That was the children's magnificent last frame ...

Conclusion to Part 1

As we suggested in our overview of Part 1, issues of multilingualism and identity can only be fully understood in the frameworks of multi-layered theoretical models from different fields, and through exploring the interplay of the local and global in practice. This part of the book has introduced us to a variety of ways in which identities are constructed, fulfilled and empowered in multilingual contexts, which have implications not just for individuals and communities but also, and even more strongly, for society and its wider interests. The chapters' journey through diverse European communities reveals examples of social responsibility and action on the one hand and ways of fulfilling identity through creativity on the other. Their content can be summarised at three main levels of understanding: community and personal, institutional, and urban.

The community and personal level: identity as a process of self-development

Young people construct their own multilingual identities in various ways, such as via bilingual theatre in London or digital photography in Cyprus. Communities can also be seen as engaging in processes of self-development at a diasporic or local level, for example the Yemeni community's initiatives in Sheffield, or the Tamil emigrants' communications via new media.

The institutional level: a two-way exchange

Constructing a multilingual identity can be assisted by interculturalisation, involving recognition by the dominant society of the identities of newcomers and facilitating contact between groups. This can lead to a two-way exchange that encourages integration. Examples of this are the schools in Barcelona and Utrecht that are successfully promoting young people's use of languages, and teachers and families working together on carnival projects in schools in London.

Multilingual cities: a sense of belonging

In some settings, institutional action receives strong support from policies at the urban level, less often acknowledged than national policies. Multilingual cities can create a sense of belonging and pride that arises from diversity for all their citizens, where all can identify as members of a diverse city population. The Utrecht Interculturalisation Policy and the Sheffield Multilingual City Initiative show how effective such an approach can be.

These two chapters affirm the possibilities to be found in actively promoting multilingualism at different and connected levels, not just for individuals or for specific communities, but for the cohesion and wellbeing of society as a whole.

Part 2:

Home, school and community

Section editors:
Charmian Kenner and Christine Hélot

Overview of Part 2

A group of mothers is clustered around a noticeboard in the reception area of an East London primary school. They have just delivered their children to class and the school corridors grow quiet as the morning's lessons begin. But the mothers are not quiet. They are chatting animatedly in Bengali, pointing to photos of a school trip displayed on the noticeboard, identifying their children in the pictures and talking about the activities involved. Most of the women are wearing the hijab (headscarf) and a couple are wearing the niqab (face-veil).

These mothers evidently feel welcome in the school. They feel comfortable about occupying this particular school space, dressed as they wish and using their own language, talking with each other about their children's learning. Such a sense of trust, enabling parents to feel at home in school, could be an essential first step in building relationships between home, school and community. Beyond this, there are many further steps a school could take in constructing a learning community, such as engaging parents in social activities, involving them as partners in their children's education, or inviting parents to join the school's governing body.

However, the concept of a learning community may be seen very differently in other European countries, or indeed in schools which are around the corner from one another. A new head teacher in another East London primary school, for example, arrived to find parents venturing no further than the school gate, and staff who talked about 'us' and 'them'. And a researcher visiting a primary school in Alsace, France, observed a mother on a street corner one block away from the school gate where a group of parents were talking together. She was wearing a hijab and probably felt she should not stay too near the school gate, in the context of recent legislation in France that forbids Muslim pupils to wear headscarves on school premises. Or she may not have known that the law does not apply to parents. And if she did not speak fluent French, how would she have access to the information sent in writing about parent-teacher meetings, election of parents' representatives and general information about the school? There are many institutionalised structures available for parents to meet with teachers in French schools, but they are highly regulated and communication is nearly always in French.

Such examples of the potential gulf between parents and school lead us to ask on whose terms the home-school relationship is constructed. Issues of power immediately come to the fore. Some languages are regarded by schools as having more power than others. Bourdieu (1991) argues that in any society, different languages or language varieties have different symbolic values which are associated with other forms of capital, economic or cultural. These values are evident in most countries in Europe, since the language of schooling is the official state language, and other languages offered in the curriculum are usually dominant European ones.

However, there are theoretical models which can help us redress the power imbalance that exists in language and literacy teaching in our schools. The Continua of Biliteracy model (Hornberger, 2003) takes an ecological approach to language, emphasising the importance of the environment and the linguistic diversity that exists within it. Creese and Martin (2003) use this model to show how power is negotiated in multilingual classrooms, and to encourage teachers to open up ideological and implementational spaces for as many languages as possible. Teachers do not necessarily have to speak all the languages of their pupils; rather, they need to welcome the linguistic and cultural competence pupils bring with them to school.

Families can become active partners in this process, if schools can draw on the 'funds of knowledge' available in children's home environments. Moll *et al* (1992) encouraged teachers of Latino students in the US to explore this concept by carrying out ethnographic studies in pupils' homes. Learning acquired in the home and community context was found to represent a major social and intellectual resource which could be brought into the classroom. Once teachers in multilingual classrooms begin to respect and value home languages and cultures, they can start to develop a more inclusive approach to teaching – for example, by giving space to different languages in classroom activities, and involving parents in designing multilingual materials.

Such approaches enable the school to become a 'community of practice' (Lave and Wenger, 1991), a social group with common goals and activities, engaging in 'situated learning' which creates shared meanings through interaction with others. Teachers will then understand that each child can be a member of several communities of practice simultaneously; for example, as well as being a pupil at school, they are also an active learner within the family, and may also attend a regular voluntary-run weekend class where they study their heritage language.

Furthermore, the school will need to be aware of the variety of people involved in children's learning at home, including family members ranging from siblings to grandparents. Intergenerational learning in informal settings tends to operate in a more flexible way than school-based teacher-student interaction. Gregory (2001:309) suggests that co-construction of learning involves a 'synergy' between the participants: 'a unique reciprocity' through which they stimulate each other's thinking. Examples include bilingual siblings 'playing school' at home, where the older sibling takes the official role of teacher, but the younger child poses questions that require ideas to be re-formulated, thus triggering additional learning for both. Learning with grandparents also involves a dynamic exchange, whereby each generation offers its skills and knowledge to the other (Kenner *et al*, 2007). By recognising the strengths of such interactions, schools could reflect on different possible ways of conducting learning.

What kinds of pedagogy can be developed that are rooted in valuing home knowledge as well as the new concepts offered at school, and that draw on continual engagement with family members, who are viewed as collaborators in the process? Dialogic learning is a possible way forward. Dialogism, or double-voicedness, was identified by Bakhtin (1981) as a characteristic of social interaction. Learning involves the words of others gradually becoming our own, such as when children voice what their teacher has said and come to an understanding of the meaning. However, the teacher-learner dialogue is not necessarily one-way. Double-voicedness also involves an interaction between speakers as they position utterances in relation to each other and borrow each other's meanings. Students, their families and their teachers can explicitly set out to challenge the power relations between them and their socially-constructed views of each other, thus creating a more equally-based 'dialogic learning'. This is particularly relevant in intercultural contexts, as the key to facilitate a mutual learning encounter which could be well-expressed in the French word *rencontre*. Each participant decentres by experiencing the views of the other (*alterité*), leading to an open-minded pedagogy founded on communicative exchange.

The theoretical concepts we have presented can aid us in understanding the potential links between home, school and community. The chapters which follow give examples from a variety of contexts in different countries, of how these links can become a reality. Chapter Three considers several possible layers of linkage: between home and school, between schools in the same area, and between teachers in different countries. Chapter Four examines policies and practices concerning parental involvement in education, particularly with regard to the linguistic and cultural content of the curriculum. Chapter Five focuses on benefits to be gained from a closer engagement between children's learning in community-run mother tongue classes and their learning in the mainstream curriculum. We conclude by reflecting on the variety of ways in which the relationship between home, school and community is viewed and realised.

3

What is a learning community?

This chapter demonstrates the potential for creating learning communities by making links at different levels: between home and school, through the need for London teachers to be aware of children's learning with grandparents; between school and school, through bridges being built between schools with different pupil populations in Utrecht; and between different countries, through a children's literature project that created an international community of practice involving pupils, teachers and teacher educators in Greece, France, Spain and the UK. In all cases, actors within each context needed to discover and value aspects of knowledge existing in the worlds of others, in order to embark on the joint construction of further learning.

Learning with grandparents in East London

Charmian Kenner, John Jessel, Mahera Ruby, Eve Gregory and Tahera Arju, Goldsmiths, University of London

> I love reading Bengali stories to them, because they love listening ...They introduce me to new things and new ways. Things have really changed ... Sahil shows me how to play cards on the computer ... I really found it fascinating. (Razia, Sahil's grandmother, talking about bringing up her British Bangladeshi grandchildren in London)

For young children growing up bilingually and biculturally in London, intergenerational exchange with grandparents is an important aspect of their learning, and in families with a history of migration this exchange is a two-way process. Grandparents provide a vital link with home language and culture, as well as giving the benefit of their life experience, whilst children often hold the key to the new language and culture through English, and to new technologies such as using the computer. Here we focus on one child, 6-year-old Sahil, and his grandmother, Razia, selected from a wider study including British Bangladeshi families in East London (Jessel *et al*, 2004; Kenner *et al*, 2007). We show how Sahil and Razia share their knowledge, with Razia taking the lead as they recite Bengali poetry together and Sahil teaching Razia how to play a card game on the computer. Finally, we discuss how schools and homes can become linked 'communities of practice' (Lave and Wenger, 1991), enabling children to bring 'funds of knowledge' (González *et al*, 2005) from home into the classroom.

Studying intergenerational learning

Parents are recognised as having an important influence on learning (Desforges and Abouchaar, 2003), but there has been little research on support given by grandparents. Our study took a sociocultural approach (Vygotsky, 1978; Rogoff, 2003; Gregory, Long and Volk, 2004) to investigate how children and grandparents shared and created knowledge through joint participation in learning events. We conducted a survey with twenty families whose 3- to 6-year-old children attended an East London primary school, to find out what activities grandparents and grandchildren did together at home. Case studies were then undertaken with nine families: six Bengali-speaking and three monolingual English-speaking, reflecting the main linguistic groups in the school. Intergenerational activities were videorecorded, and children and grandparents were interviewed and asked to make scrapbooks about what they did together.

Sahil and his grandmother Razia

Sahil, aged 6, and his two younger sisters lived with their parents and Razia, their grandmother. Like other grandparents who responded to the survey, Razia played an important part in caring for her grandchildren as their parents were busy with jobs and household responsibilities. Joint activities between Razia and the children included shopping, going to the park, reading Bengali stories and poems, which was a favourite, telling stories, singing and rhymes, computer activities, watching television or videos, playing, visiting others, talking about family members and family history, and religious activities.

Languages of learning

Although Razia had learnt some English through family interactions, she saw her role as maintaining her grandchildren's heritage language: 'I speak to them in Bengali and they speak Bengali with me'. The advantages of bilingualism could otherwise be lost, since English is becoming dominant between parents and children in second and third generation families living in London. ➡ *see also Part 1: Yemenis in Sheffield p26*. As the family was Muslim, Razia also conducted religious activities with the children in Arabic. At Sahil's primary school, learning took place through English only, so interactions with his grandmother kept open the doors to other linguistic worlds.

Bengali poetry

On one visit to the household, the researchers, who were themselves bilingual in Bengali and English, asked Sahil if he would like to read something together with his grandmother. Sahil came running back into the room with a book in his hand and stated:

Sahil: I can't find the *golpo** book but I can see the ABCD book

Researcher: Is that Bangla ABCD?

Sahil: Actually it's just *chora*, yeh yeh, it is the chora.

(*Bengali has been transliterated and is in italics.)

Here, Sahil demonstrates his 'bibliographic knowledge' (Gregory, 1996); he can distinguish between a *golpo* (Bengali story) book, an *ABCD* book (about learning the English alphabet and published in Bangladesh) and a *chora* book, a collection of rhymes or poems illustrated with pictures, popular among Bangladeshi children.

With Razia seated and Sahil standing alongside her, encircled by her arm, grandmother and grandson begin reading a favourite poem together, about how a child will plan his day from the moment he wakes up and how he will follow the wisdom of elders in the community. As well as introducing Sahil to the richness of Bengali literary language, this poem contains forms of address that show respect to elders, and the content familiarises him with his Bangladeshi cultural heritage.

As Razia begins reading the *chora*, she adopts a serious tone of voice signalling a more formal mode of learning. Sahil repeats the words immediately after her, following her cadence and rhythm and taking great care with pronunciation since this is considered important when reciting Bengali poetry. He is familiar with the poem but needs his grandmother's support to successfully produce the complex phrases. Razia employs the traditional teaching pattern of demonstrating, correcting, and clarifying meaning. At one point Sahil asks:

Sahil: *Akhane ki bole?* [What does it mean here?]

Razia: *Konta?* [Which one?]

Later, when Sahil is asked what he enjoys doing with his grandmother he replies 'she tells me what the words mean in Bengali'. Razia smiles and gives him a kiss on the cheek, content with her grandson's interest in the language of his family and community. A moment later, the following exchange occurs:

Researcher: *Dadu ki English bole?* [Does Granny speak English?]

Razia: *Na ... English pare na. ... Na bolo Dadu English pare na.* [No I don't speak English, no. ... Say Granny doesn't speak English]

Sahil: A little bit.

Despite having responded to a remark by Sahil in English immediately beforehand, Razia is determined to persist in the role of the Bengali speaker. Sahil knows his grandmother understands a good deal of English, but gives a diplomatic response, acknowledging her importance as the cultural and linguistic resource for the family.

Through this joint activity, Sahil is learning rhyme and rhythm, considered to be important building blocks for early reading competence in school. His metalinguistic knowledge is further enhanced by discussing word meanings with his grandmother in Bengali. Understanding literary language in Bengali will help Sahil tackle similar ideas in his English reading, and some of the texts he reads with Razia, such as a *Snow White* storybook in Bengali, are parallel to literature he encounters in English (Gregory *et al*, 2007). The skill of memorisation is also a useful tool to add to Sahil's school learning. Finally, by developing his ability in poetry recitation and becoming familiar with Bengali literature, Sahil will feel confident in the Bangladeshi aspects of his cultural identity, giving him security and self-esteem as a learner.

Playing cards on the computer

On another visit to Sahil's house, the researchers observed Razia and the children switching between a variety of activities: handwriting in Bengali and English, story reading in Bengali, threading beads to make necklaces, more handwriting, using the computer and finally reading a Bengali poem. Whereas Razia tended to take the lead in most of these, the initiative changed to Sahil when he sets up the card game Solitaire on the computer:

Sahil: *Asho akhane.* [Come here.]

Razia: *Oita ami akhono khelte parbo na tomi khelo.* [I cannot play that yet, you play.]

In an interview, Razia commented on the relationship between her previous knowledge and experiences now being introduced by Sahil: 'I like to take part in things they do. I find it interesting how he plays cards on the computer, when I used to play as a group manually'. She is keen to learn this new skill:

Razia: *Amake bolo tomi ki ki korso.* [Tell me what you have done.]

            Dekhi to tomi. [Let me have a look.]

            Erm bolo na Dadu ... bolo na. [Erm tell Granny ... tell me.]

Sahil: *Aita akhan rakhte ...* [This one put ...]

Razia watches with interest while Sahil tries to explain what he is doing as he repositions the cards on the computer screen.

Sahil: *Aita khotai rakhi, akhane?* [Where shall I put this, here?]

Razia: Hmm

Sahil: *Na aikhane okhane airokom kore.* [No this there like this.]

Razia: *Dadu tho computer khelte pari na tomi dekhai dou.* [Granny does not know how to play computer, you show me.]

Sahil: *Akhane akhane* [Here here]

            Ami jani ... tomi koro. [I know ... you do it.]

Razia reaches for the mouse and begins to move it while attempting to press the centre scroll wheel. Sahil places his hand on top of hers, indicating that she should click the left mouse button. He then continues to guide his grandmother's hand.

For Sahil, playing Solitaire on the computer supports his English literacy learning as he navigates to the programme, and his numeracy and categorising skills through sorting and ordering the cards. Hand-eye co-ordination and fine motor control are also fostered by using the mouse. Sahil supports Razia's learning by showing her how to operate a computerised version of a card game, and develop the skills of dragging and dropping the cards into place with the mouse.

Characteristics of intergenerational learning

Grandmother and grandson thus complemented each other's learning needs. The exchange between Razia and Sahil was typical of those we observed in all the families – whether of Bangladeshi or other cultural origin – involved in our study. We found that grandparents and children treated each other as equal partners in learning in the following ways:

■ support from grandparents made the child an expert in tasks s/he could not accomplish alone, and children also supported grandparents' learning, particularly in the use of English and in tasks involving ICT

■ joint participation was constructed by an interplay between the communicative modes of language, touch, gesture and gaze

We have called this a relationship of 'mutuality'. Children and grandparents share feelings of vulnerability arising from youth and age respectively. Grandparents also have more time for children compared to parents' busy schedules, and this tends to induce a sense of freedom and playfulness. Meanwhile, both generations show each other respect. As a result, learning happens at a relaxed tempo in a context of warmth and trust. We found physical closeness was a key aspect of the intergenerational learning relationship, with young children sitting on their grandparents' laps, putting an arm around each other or interlacing their fingers. Touch was used to shape each other's actions and to negotiate the roles of teacher and student, as we can see by comparing how Sahil and his grandmother guided each other's hands in two different contexts. Firstly, Razia placed her hand over Sahil's as he wrote in Bengali, helping him to experience how the pen flowed on the page to inscribe the pattern of each letter (Figure 3.1). A few moments later, Sahil placed his hand on top of his grandmother's to guide her in moving the mouse for the computer (Figure 3.2).

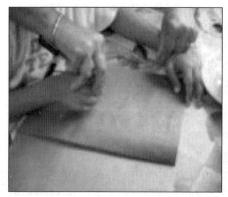

Figure 3.1: Sahil's grandmother guides his hand.

Figure 3.2: Sahil guides his grandmother's hand.

Schools and intergenerational learning

Sahil and his peers were engaged in activities at home with their grandparents that significantly complemented their learning at school. Stories and poems supported the literacy curriculum, cooking aided numeracy through weighing and measuring, and gardening fed into the science curriculum through knowledge of plant structure and growth (Ruby *et al*, 2007). Both children and grandparents held 'funds of knowledge' (González *et al*, 2005) and passed these to each other through a process of exchange, with children taking the lead where new technology was concerned.

Teachers are often unaware that children participate in such 'communities of practice' (Lave and Wenger, 1991) alongside mainstream school learning. As part of our study, the school began finding out about home activities by inviting children and their grandparents to a Grandparents' Coffee Morning. Later in the project, intergenerational learning activities were acknowledged and celebrated with families at a Grandparents' Fair. A two-way exchange of knowledge can be set up by, for example, inviting grandparents into school to share their expertise whilst also offering them access to the school's 'funds of knowledge' through computer classes. In this way, teachers can observe and learn from grandparents as well as encouraging them to participate in school life, creating a shared community of practice operating on a basis of equal respect.

World Schools: Scholen in de Wereld
Jacomine Nortier, University of Utrecht

The project Scholen in de Wereld (Schools in the World) was developed within the framework of the interculturalisation policy in Utrecht, the Netherlands, described in Part 1 of this book. Education does not only involve cognitive knowledge and skills, but also universal values such as respect, tolerance and understanding. The project contributes to developing these values by giving children the opportunity to exchange knowledge about each other's socio-cultural backgrounds.

The local government in Utrecht initiated the project in order to stimulate bidirectional integration. Whereas some schools have an exclusively native Dutch population, others are ethnically more mixed or even exclusively non-native. In the Netherlands, these schools are referred to as 'white', 'mixed' and 'black', respectively. For the sake of clarity, these terms will be used here, though readers should be aware that a 'black' school does not necessarily consist entirely of black pupils.

Schools in the World is a project where 'black', 'mixed' and 'white' schools together organise all kinds of activities to encourage integration. Examples are:

- Exchanging knowledge about socio-cultural backgrounds of different ethnic groups (at class level)
- Digital/written encounters between pupils from different types of school
- Face-to-face encounters, where one school is invited to visit the other and vice versa
- Debates about issues concerning integration
- Joint outings to relevant events
- Contributions to a video film and newsletters about Schools in the World

Since the beginning in 2003, seventeen primary schools and four secondary schools have joined the project. The goal for the years 2007-2010 is a yearly increase of four primary schools and two secondary schools. These schools are not necessarily city schools; regional schools

5. Banner headline of World Schools project newspaper.

in the province of Utrecht are allowed to participate as well. In principle, every primary or secondary school is welcome to join, and there are no restrictions as to the affiliation of the schools. In the Netherlands there are only a few private schools; the majority are public schools, and others are Protestant, Catholic, Islamic or without any religious affiliation.

In order to be recognised as a participant school, there has to be contact with other schools, and activities to stimulate interaction between pupils and their parents from different schools. In short, there are four criteria a school has to meet:

- The school has to contribute to the project's mission. The school itself is responsible for the way activities are devised and run

- The concept of being a School in the World must be embedded in the curriculum

- The project needs to be evaluated

- Parents need to be involved wherever and whenever possible

The overall effects of the project have not yet been measured. There are plans to develop a long term evaluation. What is certain is that participating schools are enthusiastic and that pupils enjoy the activities. In a recent newsletter there was an account of children from an Islamic ('black') primary school visiting a Catholic ('white') school. To give an impression of the activities within the project, this description is included and translated here:

> The children involved in this exchange were from the highest grade (eight), about 12 years old. To prepare this visit, the teachers of both schools had dinner together a few weeks earlier. Every child was linked to a child from the

other school (boy/boy, girl/girl) and the pairs had written letters to each other. Both classes had made a booklet with a photograph of the whole class and a small text written by each individual child. They had also read the other school's website. The children from the 'white' school stood outside, waiting for their visitors, and shouted with joy when they arrived. WELKOM was written on the windows! Together they sang the Worldschool song. They played games, did some craft activities and a quiz, and at noon they went to the park for a picnic with Dutch, Moroccan and Turkish food. Afterwards, both boys and girls played football.

When they were asked what they had talked about during the day, they gave some examples, such as religious celebrations which were different: Catholic children would celebrate Christmas, Muslim children would celebrate the end of Ramadan. They said that they did not expect the other children to be so much like themselves.

The teachers found this meeting beneficial, and so did the pupils and their parents.

The original name of the project, Wereldschool (World School), was changed to Scholen in de Wereld (Schools in the World) for copyright reasons.

I thank Mohamed Jaater for the time he spent explaining the details of the project to me.

Creating a community of readers across Europe: Only Connect

Christine Hélot, University of Strasbourg

The Only Connect Project is an example of a European partnership which has been running successfully for almost ten years in Greece, France, Spain and the UK. The project has involved creating links at many different levels, not only between the four countries just mentioned but also between educational partners working at different levels, from primary schools to teacher education centres and university language departments. At the heart of the project lies an interest shared by all in children's literature, a wish to discover and exchange knowledge about the wealth of our literary traditions, a curiosity about the extraordinary creativity of authors writing for children, and the idea that young pupils in our classrooms should discover books from other countries that were originally written in languages other than their own.

In the UK, children's literature in translation is sparse compared with other European countries: while European children know the most famous English authors (J.K. Rowling, Philip Pullman, Roald Dahl, Anthony Browne, Anne Fine etc), of all the material published in the English-speaking world, only 3% is translated from other languages (Bush, 2001). As renowned translator Anthea Bell observed (2001:24) 'Even with that tradition of acknowledged and continuing excellence behind it, children's literature in the United Kingdom is in something of a ghetto.' Thus from the first meeting at the University of Exeter in 1998, it was decided that the project should question on the one hand the monocultural bias of most books read in schools in the UK and on the other, the dominance of the Anglo-American market in publications for children in mainland Europe. The aim of the project was therefore to expose children in the four different countries to literature that is not usually made available to them by the publishing industry. Special care was taken in selecting books of high literary quality which dealt, to some extent, with the theme of cultural diversity, thus demonstrating how each country caters for today's multicultural society.

The project is intercultural by nature; based on the idea of using children's literature as a means to increase children's knowledge and understanding of other European countries, our perspective was to make children aware of linguistic and cultural diversity while at the same time stressing the universal values shared within a common European heritage.

The project is also multi-layered and has been structured in the following way: each year, the partners in each country select one book for readers aged eight to ten, and each book is then translated into the other three languages by university students taking translation courses in the four countries. The translation of each book is posted on the website. The following year, reading notes and pedagogical activities are produced for each book by the partners in the four education departments and posted on the website. The four books in their original language, their translations into the other three languages, and the literacy activities are then taken into schools by teachers and student teachers who read the stories with their pupils and carry out the literacy activities based on the pedagogical notes.

The pupils get a hands-on experience of linguistic diversity through the presentation of the books in their original language. They then receive an explanation of what the process of translation means and they can discover the story with their teacher. The project also aims to make them aware that there are other pupils in the countries where the books come from who are reading the same stories, and to motivate them to communicate with their peers in other European countries.

From the point of view of the partners in each country, who in some cases are language specialists and in others teacher educators, the project has given them the opportunity to exchange ideas and enter into debates on many central issues: the status of children's literature in university departments and in national curricula, the structure of teacher education, differing approaches to the teaching of literacy at primary level, and the relationship between language, culture and identity. Regarding the latter issue, what criteria should be used to choose a book which is supposed to represent Greek, Spanish, French or British culture? The following choices were made in the first year: the Greek book was a political allegory of democracy set in a classroom, the French book related the story of a little boy whose father is intent on him learning foreign languages, the book in English was a traditional Scottish story and the Spanish book a moving story of a disabled boy who learns to cope with his physical impairment.

The books were popular with the students in university departments who had to translate them. Knowing that the books had never been translated before and that their translations would be read to children the following year put them in the situation of professional translators. Particular emphasis was put on sensitivity to the cultural content of the books, for example respecting proper nouns and any specific features which might be difficult to translate but which should not lead to an adaptation. One example will illustrate this point: in the French story to be translated into English, there is a reference to identity cards which the students wanted to translate into 'passport', justifying their answers with the fact that in the UK people do not have identity cards. Of course, the expression 'identity cards' needed to be kept in English, because it would give teachers in the UK the chance to explain to their pupils that in continental Europe most people have such cards and can use them instead of passports. It could also give them the possibility to discuss a hotly debated issue in the UK. Interestingly, one French student teacher, on hearing there were no ID cards in the UK, exclaimed 'But how can they live without ID cards?'

Student translators have been encouraged to communicate with their peers in other universities through email to ask for clarifications. Thus the translation process is a first step in working with university students who, in France in particular, are going to become primary teachers, on the question of cultural stereotypes and on fostering an understanding of intercultural education. Translating a text from one language into another does not just mean transposing it, but creating a bridge between the two cultures, making a text from one culture available to another. While it is a difficult intellectual exercise, translation also demands that students de-centre themselves, that they learn to envisage the world from other points of view and reflect on how to make these points of view accessible to readers from other cultures. In this sense, translation is an intercultural activity which has broadened the outlook of student teachers in two directions: it has helped them to think about the cultural dimension in language teaching, and it has made them aware of the cultural wealth in children's literature.

The project has also motivated the French students who, when they become teachers the following year, are keen to share the stories they have translated with their pupils, and to use the other three books to introduce their pupils to selected literature from other countries. Because of their experience of communicating with other students internationally about the translation, they were keen to encourage the same experience of exchange in their classrooms, so that their pupils would share the culture of other European children through reading books in translation. For example, as a preparatory activity for reading the books, a correspondence was organised between a school in France and a school in England (Hélot, 2002). Pupils in each class were asked to write what they thought of their peers in the other country and exchanged letters. The representations on both sides of the channel included so many stereotypes that the pupils were furious and decided to write back and explain what they were really like. When they finally understood that they had more in common in their likes and dislikes, they concluded that despite some differences between their two countries, they were very similar. The books from the project were introduced at this stage.

Another year, the French book *C'est Bien*, a collection of brief stories relating what is good in a young child's everyday life, was used as a stimulus for children in the four countries to write about what was good in their own life. Some of these texts were exchanged between French children and Greek children who also found out that they had many things in common. Of course such activities require the children to write to each other in their native language and the teachers have to get help in translating the documents if they don't understand the language. However, the teacher can also use the letters or texts to make pupils aware of linguistic diversity and to explain the importance of translation as a central process for communication amongst people who do not speak the same language. We should also remember that there are many children in our classes who speak other languages at home and who act as interpreters for members of their family. This difficult and important skill should be valued in our schools and bilingual children should be made aware that they have a very special competence that enables them to help people communicate.

Up to now approximately 30 books spanning four languages have each been translated into the other three languages, and hundreds of student teachers, teachers and pupils have read them. Every year parcels travel across four countries in Europe with the new books to be translated and partners meet to put together lengthy and complicated applications to the European Commission in Brussels. Despite problems in obtaining funding for the translation part of the project, the pedagogical partners in France, Spain, Greece and the UK received several rounds of funding (through Comenius Action 2B). Two international conferences were organised in Strasbourg and Athens and were attended by some of the authors of the chosen books. Authors have also been invited to come and speak to their translators at university and their readers in schools, and a website was designed for all partners making the translations and proposed literacy activities available online.

The translation courses in children's literature are now fully integrated into the various university departments. Student teachers are delighted to be offered such a library of children's books in translation as well as useful notes which they can adapt to their particular context. Teachers love the feeling of knowing that other teachers in Greece, Spain, France or the UK are reading

6. Books from France, the UK, Greece and Spain used for the Only Connect project.

the same books to their pupils and that they strive for the same aims: less prejudice and intolerance and more shared understandings. Teacher educators
are convinced such a project helps future teachers to understand that literature is a shared way of interpreting the world and that the experience of
otherness is at the heart of the creative process. As for the children, most importantly, they enjoy the stories, they are fascinated by the different languages
(and script in the case of Greek), and they love to discover a world which can
at times be familiar to them and at others very strange. They love the humour
of some authors and the poetry of others, they understand the sadness of
grandparents dying and of parents divorcing, they feel for the cat which has
been left behind during the heat-wave while the family goes on holiday and
the dog being badly treated in the streets of Paris, because all these stories
transcend national boundaries. What the Only Connect project has done is to
break down language barriers and make stories available across four European countries to children and teachers who can now share their enjoyment
of reading.

Address of website: https://webct.st-and.ac.uk/public/EC001/

4
Links between schools and families

The projects presented in Chapter Four show how schools can link directly with parents and other family members. In Utrecht, parents were invited to learn how the education system works and become involved with the governance of their children's schools. Such a step paves the way for dialogic exchange. Research in Swedish pre-schools went one step further, seeking parents' views on whether and how the curriculum should involve mother tongue. Finally, action research in a French primary school led to even fuller engagement with parents as they worked dialogically with teachers, drawing on funds of knowledge about languages and cultures and thus changing power relationships in the classroom.

Every Parent Counts
Jacomine Nortier, University of Utrecht

The multiethnic context in Utrecht was discussed in Part 1, together with the municipality's policy of 'interculturalisation'. This approach to multiculturalism aims to promote encounters between native Dutch and non-native citizens so that people come to understand each other's cultural backgrounds, and integration is thus a bi-directional process. Here I describe the Every Parent Counts project and explain how it fits within the interculturalisation approach.

Schools in the Netherlands have advisory boards and parents' councils. Advisory boards are slightly higher-level and more powerful than parents' councils; other members such as teachers and policy makers participate in them as well as parents. Almost all the parents on most advisory boards and many parents' councils had a native Dutch background, even when the school's population was ethnically diverse. In order to change this situation, Every Parent Counts came into being in 2000. The project was subsidised by the Utrecht municipal fund for Social Integration and supported by the municipal department of social development. Every Parent Counts was scheduled to run for a period of three years in eight or nine districts in Utrecht. The project's goal was to strengthen the position of parents by spreading knowledge about parent participation, and to train parents who had not previously been involved to become members of the advisory board or parents' council of their children's primary school.

Parents were approached through participating schools, and grass-roots organisations and community leaders were involved in identifying potential candidates. In this process of finding and selecting participants, the Utrecht Multicultural Institute, a community workers' organisation, played a helpful role. The most important criterion potential participants had to meet was oral and written proficiency in Dutch, irrespective of ethnic background. Both native Dutch and candidates with a migrant background participated. They had a common interest at heart: the quality of their children's schools.

The courses were run by professional trainers from *Kerk en Wereld* (Church and World, an institute for dialogue, research and training in the field of social issues) and consisted of six meetings plus a weekend training. Topics included the development of skills such as organising meetings, giving presentations and taking minutes, gaining insight into the Dutch educational system, and dealing with differences. Parents who were already members of advisory boards were invited to participate to offer insights from practical experience. After a final evaluation, certificates were handed out at a celebration event.

Effects

The course proved very useful for parents who wanted to develop their skills and broaden their vision on matters such as pre-school daycare, the community functions of schools and different approaches to teaching and learning.

The course was evaluated several times and improved accordingly. In the beginning a few problems arose. For example, some native Dutch participants complained and eventually left because of the slow pace of exchanges due to participants whose first language was not Dutch. Another problem was to keep peoplc involved and interested in issues raised by participants from ethnic backgrounds other than their own. Those who stayed thought the course had been good. After running for two years it had become truly intercultural, with a growing number of participants.

The course quickly proved to have positive outcomes. Participants reported being more assertive and more involved, not only in their children's school activities but also at work. They learned from advisory boards of other schools they came into contact with during the course. And they had learned to communicate with other parents in a more effective way. Long-term effects were even more promising. Participants were more inclined to become members of advisory boards, or to switch from parents' councils to the more powerful advisory boards.

Challenges raised by the project

One of the main migrant groups that participated in the project was the Turkish community. People of Turkish origin in the Netherlands have a strong orientation towards their own group, and second generation young people continue to use Turkish as well as Dutch. This can be seen on their internet sites such as www.turksestudent.nl and www.lokum.nl, where a mix of Dutch and Turkish is common.

Within Every Parent Counts, Turkish participants expressed a clear preference for having a specific Turkish section. As well as participating in the project, Turkish parent committees initiated training and courses in Turkish, for Turkish parents only. The Turkish-only courses were not part of the original plans and did not fit within the philosophy of interculturalisation. On the other hand, these courses enabled vulnerable members of Every Parent Counts to find strength and protection in their own group and through using their own language. Minority groups may need to first strengthen their own identity before they can open up to the dominant culture and then to other ethnic groups. As long as this approach leads to more participation in advisory boards and parents' councils, it can ultimately be seen as empowering these parents and therefore as a successful adaptation of the project.

Thanks to Mohamed Jaater for information on the project.

Multilingual pre-schools in Sweden:
Finding out what parents really want
Monica Axelsson, University of Stockholm

The Swedish pre-school has been part of the country's well-developed welfare system since the 1980s. Since most parents work outside the home, and women are accorded equal rights in the workplace, pre-schools in Sweden have expanded tremendously. Although not compulsory, they currently welcome about 94% of all young children. For children born outside Sweden or having two parents born outside Sweden the designation 'foreign background' is used, and this group amounts to 15% of all children between 1 and 5 years old. However, in some urban areas up to 100% of the children in pre-school are multilingual, particularly in suburbs around Stockholm, Göteborg and Malmö.

Multilingualism in education in Sweden

Since 1977, Sweden has had a law explicitly supporting the goal of active bilingualism. There is a right to instruction in mother tongue for a maximum period of seven years if there are 5 children or more in a municipality who share a language. There are no restrictions on the numbers needed for the national minority languages Sami, Finnish, Meänkieli, Romani Chib and Yiddish. Some bilingual groups have started their own schools, such as Swedish/Finnish and Swedish/Arabic schools. Meanwhile, since 1995 Swedish as a Second Language (SSL) has had a parallel curriculum to Swedish, qualifying students to continue to high school and university. Various models for this instruction exist, but currently there is a national trend towards integrating SSL into the mainstream through cooperation between subject teachers and SSL teachers, thus trying to support second language learners in their enormous task of developing academic language.

Since 1998 the national curriculum for pre-school has referred to the benefits of bilingualism for learning and for identity, stating that:

> Language and learning are intimately connected as are language and identity development. Pre-school should pay close attention to stimulating each child's language development, encouraging and fostering the child's curiosity and interest in literacy. Pre-school should contribute to the possibilities for children with a mother tongue other than Swedish to develop both Swedish and their mother tongue. (*Läroplan för förskolan Lpfö*, 1998:10)

However, teacher education courses on bilingualism are scarce, resulting in few teachers trained in SSL or bilingualism. In Stockholm the municipality has educated about 300 pre-school and school teachers through the university course The Development of Language, Cognition and Academic Proficiency of Bilingual Children, thus raising teachers' awareness about bilingual language acquisition and academic achievement. ➡ *see also Part 3: Learning and teaching for bilingual children p158.*

Academic achievement is an important issue since statistics over several years show that after Grade 9 (age 15) about 9% of the monolingual Swedish students are unable to continue to mainstream national programmes in high school – but this rises to about 20% for bilingual students. Bilingual experiments have therefore been considered and in Stockholm bilingual maths classes have been successfully run for a couple of years in Arabic and Somali. Politically, mother tongue instruction as an educational resource seems to be favoured and Parliament has just extended the permission for experimental bilingual instruction in schools until 2009.

The multilingual pre-school

A study was conducted in a pre-school mainly comprising multilingual children (Axelsson, 2005). All sixteen children in the focus group were aged 5 and were from bilingual backgrounds. The languages represented were: Arabic (4), Somali (2), South-Kurdish (3), Tigrinya (2), Bengali (1), English (1), French (1), Lingala (1) and Indonesian (1). Except for Indonesian, all these languages were in regular use in the children's lives. In addition, two of the children spoke Swedish at home as one of their first languages. All the children except one had entered pre-school at the age of one. This is common in Sweden since most parents work outside the home, or if they are unemployed and get welfare benefits they are obliged to leave their child at pre-school in order to be available for work. The aim of the study was to investigate how multilingual children are socialised into literacy in pre-school and at home. Data were collected in the pre-school over one year, through weekly observations, video and audio recordings, interviews with parents and regular informal conversations with the pre-school teachers.

Results showed plenty of interaction between children around literacy. Children were 'reading' pictures in books, discussing content and words in stories, noticing which letters were used, talking about their own experiences, dramatising, retelling and drawing stories. But very little took place in mother tongue. During the year of the study the children's mother tongues were used or referred to on only thirteen occasions. On one occasion for example, a child was 'pretend-reading' *Pippi Longstocking* (a well-known Swedish children's book) in her mother tongue, Sorani, and asked 'how can it be in

Sorani if Astrid Lindgren (the author) is Swedish'? The teacher explained the idea of translation. On another occasion a teacher discussed with children how Arabic was written from right to left and Swedish the other way round. Both examples show that even if bilingual activities were scarce in pre-school, children were reflecting on their bilingualism. The limited extent of mother tongue activities was discussed with the pre-school teachers during the study and this resulted in invitations to parents, of whom two came and led activities in their respective mother tongues with groups of children.

Another restriction affecting literacy was the small number of genres offered to children. The main texts on offer were storybooks comprising narratives within a Swedish cultural sphere. These story and picturebooks were placed in reading corners with bookshelves and comfortable sofas. However, there were few writing areas in the pre-school, and pencils were provided mainly for colouring. Historically, activities in Swedish pre-schools are expected not to be school-like. Based on a maturational view on learning to read and write, pre-schools have not been permitted to engage in writing activities.

Parents' views

The parents interviewed were eager to socialise their children in their mother tongue and also keen that they learn Swedish. All were using mother tongue at home and requiring their children to reply in the same language. One father commented that the pre-school teachers had informed him about the importance of parents using mother tongue with their children. Parents also regularly communicated in mother tongue with extended families and com-munities, via internet, phone or letters. They watched TV in both languages, and read the free *Metro* newspaper in Swedish.

Parents were happy that pre-school was in Swedish so that their children could learn the language. However, they missed the storytelling that used to be offered in mother tongue at the community library. All planned to ask for mother tongue instruction once children reached the age of 6. Keen for their children to learn different languages, they had ideas such as encouraging them to write, using books, computers and TV.

Even though all parents expressed positive views on mother tongue main-tenance, it was obvious from interviews and observations that the children's level of bilingualism varied. In Ari's home (Table 4.1) the mother reported that South-Kurdish was mainly used. Parents and older relatives addressed Ari in South-Kurdish and accordingly he replied in the same language. This active and dominant use of the mother tongue in Ari's home is most probably why

Ari was one of the three children in the study (out of sixteen in all) who spontaneously used mother tongue in pre-school.

Table 4.1 Language use in Ari's home as reported by parent

Relative	Spoke language X to	Child	Spoke X to	Relative
Mother	South-Kurdish	Ari	South-Kurdish	Mother
Father	South-Kurdish	Ari	South-Kurdish	Father
Younger sister (age 1)	South-Kurdish	Ari	South-Kurdish	Younger sister (Age 1)
Cousin (age 7)	Swedish	Ari	Swedish/ South-Kurdish	Cousin (Age 7)
Older relatives	South-Kurdish	Ari	South-Kurdish	Older relatives

Table 4.2 Language use in Ayhan's home as reported by parent

Relative	Spoke language X to	Child	Spoke X to	Relative
Mother	Arabic, sometimes Swedish	Ayhan	Swedish	Mother
Father	Arabic	Ayhan	Swedish	Father
Older brother	Swedish	Ayhan	Swedish	Older brother
Relatives	Arabic	Ayhan	Swedish	Relatives

Table 4.3 Language use in Nuri's home as reported by parent

Relative	Spoke language X to	Child	Spoke X to	Relative
Mother	Tigrinya/Swedish	Nuri	Swedish	Mother
Father	Tigrinya	Nuri	Swedish	Father
Younger sister	Swedish	Nuri	Swedish	Younger sister
Adult relatives	Swedish	Nuri	Swedish	Adult relatives

In Ayhan's and Nuri's homes, as shown by the tables above, Swedish was the stronger language, especially for the children, and neither Ayhan nor Nuri ever used mother tongue in pre-school. Despite this dominance of Swedish, Ayhan discussed the difference in reading direction between Swedish and Arabic on repeated occasions, indicating his awareness of both languages. Nuri's parents came to Sweden via Italy from Eritrea. In Italy they spoke Italian at school, and it was only when they came to Sweden that they discovered a strong Tigrinya community in the area where they lived and started to speak Tigrinya again. Now they are eager for Nuri to develop his mother tongue, and on Saturdays he goes to the local Tigrinya school.

Key factors affecting children's bilingualism

The study found that the key factors affecting children's bilingualism were:

The children's age when they start pre-school

Nearly all children studied began pre-school around 12 months, so they had not yet started to speak their mother tongue fluently before spending five to eight hours a day, five days a week in a Swedish dominant environment. Together with the finding that mother tongue usage in the families varied a lot, it is obvious that the early start in pre-school endangered the development of the children's first language.

The need for parent-school communication

While differing in their efforts to enhance mother tongue at home, all the parents interviewed expressed a wish for their children to be bilingual. It is unclear, however, whether this wish had been overtly stated to the pre-school, since the head of pre-school believed that parents were content, and interpreted this as meaning that they only wanted Swedish for their children. Pre-school teachers therefore left the responsibility for mother tongue to parents.

The limited range of genres and scripts

Besides the limited use of mother tongue in pre-school, there was also a genre limitation since most texts were narratives, connected to Swedish culture and in Latin script. Writing activities were also few and usually took place only in one script. As a result, although children developed a near-native proficiency in Swedish by the age of five and displayed well-developed literacy skills in Swedish, they were unable to develop similar proficiency in mother tongue.

Changing pre-school practice

Results from the study have been widely disseminated and discussed, especially in Stockholm, and pre-school teachers all over the city have started to develop activities supporting children's mother tongues. Adhering to the law concerning active bilingualism, inventories of staff bilingual proficiency have been made, resulting in mother tongue groups being formed for meals and school trips. More multilingual pre-schools have bought children's books in the various languages represented, and stories have been tape-recorded in the most commonly-used languages for children to listen to on an individual basis. In some pre-schools, parents or pupils from nearby schools have been invited to come and read stories to children in their respective mother tongues. Such activities have created bonds between children of different ages, enhancing pupils' reading proficiency and mother tongue for all participants. Parents have started to take a more active interest in the pre-school as they see how their children develop both languages. Bilingual children have been encouraged to retell stories in both their languages and their stories have been written down for teachers and parents to compare.

Slowly, pre-school teachers have started to become aware of the need to incorporate the children's full language repertoire in the development of literacy and knowledge about the world. In sum, these efforts give visibility and legitimacy to other languages as well as Swedish in the multilingual pre-school.

Parent-teacher partnerships:
Co-constructing knowledge about languages
and cultures in a French primary school
Andrea Young and Christine Hélot,
University of Strasbourg/ IUFM

All families care about the physical, mental and emotional well-being of their children. Sometimes lack of parental participation in school matters is misconstrued by school staff as lack of interest in a child's education. The extent of parental involvement in school activities is governed by many varied constraints such as work, family, time, transport or finance. For parents who belong to a culture other than the mainstream and speak a language other than the dominant one, taking on an active role in their child's education can be doubly challenging as they may have to overcome both linguistic and cultural barriers at school.

The French context

In France, parental involvement in school is dealt with, like everything else, in a series of texts from the Ministry of Education in Paris (MEN, 2006). These texts state that parents have the right to be informed about their child's results and behaviour, they may request an individual meeting with a teacher, and parent-teacher meetings should be held at least twice a year. During these meetings parents may be informed about new legislation, examinations, curricula etc and can give their opinions and sometimes influence the functioning of the school. However, the education system traditionally adheres to a top-down model and the reality of official ministerial policy confines parental participation to a rather rigid framework which seeks to regulate direct contact between teachers and families through parent representatives and parent associations.

The Ministry has also pointed out that 'It is important to facilitate exchanges with parents who are not familiar with such meetings or who do not master the French language well' (Debbasch, 2006). However, practical advice as to how to facilitate such exchanges is not provided. The text continues 'Dialogue with parents of pupils is based upon the mutual recognition of one another's skills and roles (the professionalism of the teachers within the framework of their work, the educational responsibilities of the parents)' (*ibid*).

The underlying belief that teachers and parents should move in separate spheres, the former being responsible for the instruction of pupils and the latter for the general education of their children, is nothing new in France. It is one of a series of legacies inherited from the free secular republican system of education established by Jules Ferry in the late nineteenth century. At that time the French population was largely rural, spoke a variety of regional languages and received very little formal education outside the teachings of the Catholic Church. Free compulsory schooling for all was identified as the primary means of strengthening the nation state. Schools would produce French citizens. *Laïcité* (secularism) and *égalité* (equal opportunities) were to be the watchwords of the education system and still are. Pupils would be protected from outside influences such as the Church, and family background and privileges were to be banished from the classroom with the intention of giving all pupils an equal start in life. The shared language of the nation and of education was to be standard French. Regional languages were subsequently equated with backwardness. In this context, the school teacher became a leading member of the local community, revered by families and seen as a knowledgeable model citizen playing a key role in leading the nation towards progress and modernity (Prost, 2006).

Since that time France has moved on but along a continuum, evolving gradually. Parents' associations began to develop in the 1960s as a move to redress the balance of power, but the relationship between teachers and parents remains rather formal and distant, sometimes marked by lack of trust and in some cases by lack of respect. True home-school educational partnership initiatives are thus relatively rare in France, with each party tending to keep to their own territory, the professional or the parental. Furthermore, as France has become a more multicultural society, the concept of treating all children as 'the same' and ignoring different family backgrounds has become seriously problematic. Parents from cultures other than the mainstream are far less likely to request a meeting with their child's teacher or become involved in parent associations.

The Didenheim Project

Within the French context, the Didenheim project is a rare example of a successful collaboration between two teachers and a group of parents and community members, some of them originating from other countries, in a small primary school in the south of Alsace. This innovative initiative began as a three year school project but is now part of the regular school curriculum (Hélot and Young, 2006). Following a number of racist incidents at school, teaching staff decided to make education about languages and cultures pivotal to their school project. The aims of the programme were:

> to bring the children into contact with other languages and to sensitise them to the use of languages, to familiarise the children with other cultures through the presentation of festivals, traditions, costumes, geography [...], and last but not least to promote the acceptance of differences, to learn about others and to attempt to break down stereotypical misconceptions (minutes from school project meeting, 7/10/00).

Between 2000 and 2003, all pupils in the first three classes (aged 6-10) were introduced to a total of eighteen languages and cultures, including local regional varieties, majority and minority European ones, those brought to Alsace through migration and French Sign Language. This rich linguistic and cultural diversity contrasted starkly with the school's limited linguistic repertoire at that time which amounted to French as the language of instruction, German or English as a foreign language for one and a half hours a week for the older pupils (aged 9-11) and Arabic, Polish and Turkish as options for a small minority of children. Many languages present in the local community did not have a place at school. The few languages which were accorded a legitimate space in the school timetable were quite obviously regarded by the pupils as separate entities, having little or no connection between one another. The project endeavoured to build bridges between languages, placing them all on an equal footing, and prompted such questions as 'Is French a language too then?' from one 9-year-old pupil.

The content of the project was co-constructed by parents and teachers, the teachers contributing their pedagogical experience, the parents their cultural knowledge and linguistic skills (Young, 2007; Young and Hélot, 2007). Activities have included:

- the learning and singing of short songs and rhymes in another language
- learning about geography and history of different countries
- using different written scripts
- comparing and contrasting linguistic features of different languages
- tasting and learning about specialities from different culinary traditions
- listening to traditional tales read from bilingual books
- learning traditional dances
- talking about lifestyles and living conditions in different countries
- learning how to introduce oneself, greet and say please and thank you in context
- basic vocabulary such as colours or fruits.

All sessions are jointly planned by parents and teachers and run by the parents with the teacher participating alongside pupils as a learner.

Opening the doors of the school to parents was already part of Didenheim's practices. Parents were regularly invited to help out with practical classes at school such as art, accompanying school trips and swimming lessons, but some parents could not be enticed to cross the frontier from home to school. This was noticeably the case for parents who had recently arrived from other countries. Although the teachers were used to working with parents, they had never before stepped back to allow parents to take the lead in teaching activities. The project provided both parents and teachers with a legitimate framework which allowed them to recognise one another's skills, knowledge and experience and to work together as equal educational partners (Cummins, 2001).

Parents and children sometimes adopted the role of teachers, whilst teachers momentarily became learners alongside their pupils, intervening only occasionally to lend pedagogical or logistical support to the parent. The teachers acknowledged that parental skills and knowledge complemented their own professional experience. One said:

> I don't think it bothers me to have anyone in my class ... so long as I think it is legitimate, I myself was in the situation of the learner for some languages ... I don't think that I know all there is to know about all the cultures and languages which we have looked at ... as for classroom management that's my job.

Chanson: **SANT NIKOLAUS**
(SAINT NICOLAS)

Refrain:

Sant Nikolaus, kumsch noch net ?
(Saint Nicolas ne viens-tu pas encore ?)

Ich hab so langi Zitt !
(Je m'impatiente tant !)

Was bringsch fer Gschankla met ?
(Qu'apportes-tu comme cadeaux ?)

Ich wart, vergess mich net !
(J'attends, ne m'oublie pas !)

7. Song in Alsatian dialect with French translation.

93

Another spoke of how the collaborative partnerships had led to professional and personal development: 'A huge opening up, you know, an even greater desire to discover other languages, other countries. A boundless curiosity ...'. The pupils appeared to appreciate both the authentic dimension of parental participation in classes and the limitations of their class teacher, making comments such as: 'It's better when it's other people in the class because the teacher cannot come from all those countries', 'we understand better when it's people from outside who come to present their languages', 'I enjoyed people coming to our class because the teacher hardly knows any languages', and 'my mummy knows more than the teacher'.

'The school walls have come down' was how one of the Didenheim teachers described the consequences of letting the outside world into the school. Parents were pleasantly surprised by this breaking down of barriers. One Turkish mother talking about the Turkish community's reactions to the project said: 'they are happy and they are shocked ... especially that we are giving the lessons, we are foreigners and then they see that in Didenheim they are not like that ...' (ie the school is welcoming to different cultures). All the parents who participated in the project were extremely positive about the experience. Valuing diversity as a resource and viewing pupils' families as repositories of funds of knowledge (González *et al*, 2005) has undoubtedly improved home school relations in Didenheim. One teacher commented 'It's fantastic, I have superb relationships with these mothers.' Another teacher told of how an Arabic speaking mother had said that 'she had felt good about presenting her culture ... presenting another side of her culture ... it made her feel valued I think and she needed that.'

Minority pupils and their families can often feel torn between two cultures, between allegiance to family traditions and values and pressure to conform to the majority culture in the country in which they are living. For many, the desire and the need to integrate into mainstream society is so strong that they feel obliged to abandon part of their identity in order to become accepted. The teachers in Didenheim referred to this unspoken pressure when discussing how their pupils had never even objected to the mispronunciation of their names: 'they're kids, they daren't say it, you can see the crushing of their foreign culture there, not being able to say 'no, you don't say my name like that' it hurts somehow doesn't it, because having two different names, one at school with the French and one at home...'. One second generation Berber parent spoke of her own family culture and school days in France: 'whereas at the time I thought it was a sub-culture, perhaps it was the school system which made us think that, the people and everything that made us think that

Arabic wasn't ...'. She went on to say that she hoped that the project in Didenheim would present the children with 'another vision of things ... an open-mindedness ... an opening up to others, tolerance, greater tolerance, something I didn't experience at school.'

The work carried out in Didenheim was innovatory as it has successfully challenged three salient features present in many French primary schools today, but whose roots lie firmly in the past:

- an absence of outsiders, including parents, inside many primary schools
- a refusal to recognise the diverse cultural identities of individual pupils
- a belief that the only legitimate language at school is the language of the Republic, French

The parents and teachers in Didenheim are overcoming linguistic and cultural barriers and working together as equal members of the educational community by pooling their resources and according each other the respect they all deserve.

5

Links between complementary and mainstream schools

Chapter Five reveals the learning taking place in after-school and weekend language classes which act as parallel communities of practice, complementing mainstream education, and are therefore often called complementary schools. For example, children in London gain additional knowledge and strategies for learning by attending Portuguese classes or Chinese school. A project in Bradford, Northern England, links mainstream and out-of-school communities of practice, thus directly uniting children's funds of knowledge. However, even when community classes are run on mainstream school premises, the link can be fragile unless minority languages and cultures are truly valued by the school authorities and wider society, as shown here in the account of a campaign against the closure of Turkish classes at Dutch schools.

How Portuguese and Chinese community schools support educational achievement
Olga Barradas and Yangguang Chen,
Goldsmiths, University of London

Children of Chinese origin out-perform all other children in UK schools. Community-organised Chinese classes have been suggested as one factor contributing to this success (Francis and Archer 2005; Chen, 2007). Meanwhile, Portuguese children who attend after-school Portuguese classes obtain better results in UK schools than those who do not (Barradas, 2004). Here we explore the pivotal role that community language schools play in supporting achievement through establishing a learning community between parents and children, thus enabling transmission of language and culture and the construction of ethnic identity.

Community schools have a long history in the UK. The first Chinese class in London dates from 1928. Chinese schools expanded in the late 1960s and early 1970s, and there are now over 2000 across the country, generally taking place on Saturdays and Sundays. Portuguese migrants began organising classes in a community hall in London in the 1960s. Since 1974, the Portuguese government has recruited and paid teachers for classes currently attended by over 3000 students in several UK locations, usually after school in classrooms hired from mainstream schools.

Although a European Economic Community directive (EEC, 1977) required the provision of mother tongue maintenance classes for children of immigrant origin in the UK, the Swann Report (DES, 1985) stated this was the responsibility of communities themselves rather than the government. A powerful motivation behind the continuing existence of community classes has been the desire to maintain linguistic and cultural heritage, and communication between the generations, as illustrated by these quotations (see Barradas, 2007:91):

> I think that it is very important that a person put their children to learn Portuguese, because many Portuguese children cannot speak Portuguese. Especially those that were born here. The parents have to work, and they have to leave their children with minders and normally, those are people that speak in English to them. Of course, the children will begin to learn the English language, not the Portuguese. Although they speak Portuguese at home, but it is so little. It is not enough to learn (...) I think it is important that our children learn the same language as their parents. For me, I think that is very important because- it is a very beautiful language. (Carlos's Mother)
>
> If I didn't know how to speak Portuguese, how could I communicate with my mum? (Joana)

Portuguese classes: the root of achievement

Children can attend Portuguese classes between the ages of 6 and 18, during which time they can take nationally recognised GCSE and A-level qualifications in the language. The reasons given by both parents and students for attendance focus on cultural identity and affective links with family in the UK and in Portugal. Parents also regard these classes as an academic investment to be reaped in the future, and therefore the earlier children start the better.

As Carmina's mother puts it: 'I think that for us, to learn a little bit of everything, it doesn't harm anyone'. She contrasts her attitude with that of other parents who don't enrol their children in Portuguese classes: 'because they think that knowing English they have everything in life' ... they say 'They know English. What are they going to need the Portuguese for?' '

Meanwhile, for the children, Portuguese classes offer a welcoming environment where they can develop self-esteem and a sense of achievement. Norberto comments: 'It's good. Because sometimes you have good work and I am the first to finish. And sometimes I'm there trying to see if I can do it. And I do it. I don't need help.'

The academic content of mother tongue classes has a strong focus on literacy skills. The classes are taught by qualified teachers, mostly using age-appropriate textbooks for the mainstream classroom in Portugal. In the primary years, literacy work generally takes on the typical Portuguese format of text, sentence and word analysis. As the teachers are bilingual, this often involves comparing Portuguese and English, thus developing students' metalinguistic skills through grammatical awareness and knowledge of terminology such as prefix and suffix, and enriching vocabulary through in-depth discussion of word meanings.

8. Ines, aged 9, describes her village of origin in Portugal.

A Vila de Galveias, Portugal

Eu gosto de Galveias porque a vila é pequena e tudo fica perto de casa.
A minha avó tem uma casa grande com laranjeiras no jardim.
Tem um parque com um lago e baloiços e eu tenho amigos Portugueses em Galveias.

Ines 9anos

As well as linguistic development, the curriculum includes the geography and history of Portugal. Children become familiar with cultural aspects of various regions of Portugal and their traditions and events, whilst studying the history of the country. This approach allows children to look at historical facts through different perspectives and develop a critical appreciation of them. Thus, they are not only learning abstract concepts, but also culturally relevant ideas that they can relate to. They are required to compare, criticise, discuss, extrapolate and analyse different viewpoints and approaches to knowledge.

As a result, children attending Portuguese classes are more likely to achieve higher results in mainstream school. In a study of Portuguese 16-year-olds in London (Barradas, 2004), 41% of students attending Portuguese classes achieved five or more GCSE passes at grades A* to C, compared with only 8% of the students not attending.

In the case of Portuguese classes, several factors combine to affect the academic performance and development of students of Portuguese origin. Parental involvement in children's education is facilitated in an environment where they can communicate with teachers without language or cultural barriers, and relate easily to textbooks and other school materials brought home. This involvement in academic activities raises parents' awareness of their children's abilities and contributes to increased expectations regarding achievement. This achievement is upheld and furthered by academic and cognitive development in a culturally sympathetic setting.

How young people learn from their Chinese community schools

In this section we hear from five students aged 13 to 15: Susan Wu, Joyce Chen, Nicola Xian, Ying Ma and Joe Lin. They all arrived in the UK with their parents when they were around 7 to 9 years old, and mainly speak Chinese at home. Each came to London Mandarin School or Republic Chinese School to continue their literacy development in Chinese and participate in extra-curricular activities. Being brought up in a bilingual environment, they are fluent in both languages. They recently obtained the top grade of A* in GCSE Chinese, and also achieved exceptional GCSE grades in other subjects in their English school.

London Mandarin School was set up only six years ago and opens every Sunday, while Republic Chinese School has existed for nearly twenty years and runs on Saturday. Due to lack of funding, London Mandarin School has changed site several times, from a church to a business college and then a primary school. The school attracts children from all over London. In contrast,

Republic Chinese School has a permanent base in an adult education college near Central London's Chinatown, and is funded by the local Chinese community centre. Children like to drop in at the Centre before and after class, to watch videos and play table tennis or chess, and they never miss the annual festival celebration parties.

London Mandarin School teaches in Mandarin and Republic Chinese School in Cantonese. To meet the needs of pupils growing up in Britain, English is used in addition to Chinese. Bilingual teaching attracts a wider group of children of Chinese origin and also English-Chinese mixed families.

Most teachers in these two schools are parents themselves. In the Republic School, they came as students from Hong Kong and are now UK citizens working in various professions, while in London Mandarin School, they are from mainland China and first came to the UK as students and scholars. Being bilingual and having experienced life in Britain, all are aware of cultural conflicts that children of Chinese origin may face. They can therefore help to alleviate some of the 'culture shock' problems that can occur between parents and children.

The two schools have similar aims:

- to provide Chinese language teaching for children of Chinese origin
- to educate children about Chinese culture and history
- to pass on to younger generations various aspects of Chinese values and a sense of identity
- to bridge the gap between parents and their children in communication as well as in views and beliefs
- to supplement mainstream schooling by providing extra lessons in various core subjects (English, Mathematics and Science) at GCSE and A level

Sense of Chinese identity and cultural heritage

The young people participating in this study appreciated the opportunity to explore Chinese language and culture. As Joe Lin commented:

> Studying Chinese is part of our heritage and there is an added motivation to do well if we have an innate sense of identity developed through the language learning. The Chinese school has allowed us to interact with other people our age who share our culture and linguistic background.

Attitudes and commitment

Chinese school reinforced the value system exemplified in parents' hard-working lifestyles, and the young people found that such values enhanced their achievement. Nicola Xiang explained:

> Our Chinese lessons have taught us to 'work hard and aim high', which has manifested itself in many Chinese parents abroad ... This dedication has evolved into a routine of early revision resulting in better grades. This sense of self-motivation is encouraged by parents who see education as being of paramount importance to a child's development.

Knowledge and skills

The young people pointed out that extra tuition at Chinese school directly supported their mainstream school learning. Susan Wu chose her Chinese school:

> because they provide GCSE courses not only for the Chinese language, but for maths and science revision as well. Teachers are researchers themselves at the university in London ... so they know very well both the subject and the test requirement.

Joe Lin found that Chinese school had given him extra support in English, crucial for his social and academic development in mainstream school:

> At that time I was often teased and pushed around by some classmates simply because I was not yet fluent in English ... and also wronged by teachers in the school because I have no way to defend myself ...[At London Mandarin School] I could learn English from a bilingual teacher and make friends with my classmates who share with me the same learning experience.

Ying Ma highlighted the value of extra-curricular activities at Chinese school for a well-rounded education:

> There is a wide range of optional courses to attract our interest, for instance, chess club, calligraphy group, dancing class, Chinese painting lesson, Kung Fu workshop etc are very popular among both parents and students ... I think all these activities encourage us to adopt a more balanced attitude toward our learning.

Methodology and approaches to learning

Chinese school provided additional strategies that strengthened students' all-round capacities as learners. Susan Wu suggested that:

> Chinese being a character based language stimulates a different area of brain activity to when English is being used, so this may have a positive influence on our capacity to reason in different ways and to consider a question from different angles.

102

Nicola Xiang emphasised the advantages of bilingual teaching at Chinese school: 'Content and language integrated learning are encouraged, and through back and forth translation practice, our bilingual capacity has been improved.'

By combining strategies from Chinese school with the 'child-centred' approach promoted at mainstream school, students could gain the maximum advantage, as Joyce Chen explained:

> Reciting and memorising words and facts play a large part in the Chinese education system; however it is coupled with understanding, logical reasoning and application of knowledge rather than just regurgitating facts. Our Chinese lessons at the London Mandarin School have taught us to combine a creative approach and self-discovery that enable us to utilise a variety of approaches creating greater flexibility and ultimately academic success.

Conclusion

Portuguese and Chinese community schools are highly valued by parents and children alike, as an important resource contributing to ethnic and cultural identity as well as academic achievement. This type of education can serve as a significant link in a partnership between home, community and mainstream education, whilst helping maintain communication between generations. Parents feel strongly that only through knowledge of the language, and thereby the history, culture and literature, can children have a true understanding of their parents' attitudes, standards and values. Through community schools, parents are therefore directly involved in their children's education, in an academic setting whose cultural values they share. The schools serve as a bridge between parents and children, between two languages and cultures. Furthermore, through the work done at Portuguese and Chinese schools, students are able to deepen and broaden skills and knowledge they can transfer into mainstream education, allowing them to achieve academic success.

Bilingual teachers as agents of social change:
Linking the community and the mainstream
Jean Conteh, University of Leeds and Shila Begum,
Bilingual Learning and Teaching Association

The city of Bradford has a long history of linguistic, cultural and religious diversity. For hundreds of years, groups of migrants from all over the world, seeking work in the textile mills or to trade in the fabrics they produced, have settled there. Each formed their own distinctive community, adding to the richness and complexity of the life of the city, and in recent years the teaching staff in Bradford schools has begun to reflect this ethnic diversity.

The beginning of the Bilingual Learning and Teaching Association (BLTA)

In 2003, two members of one of the largest minority ethnic communities in Bradford, of Pakistani heritage, completed their training as primary teachers. Saiqa Riasat and Reefath Rehman were both Language and Literature specialists and bilingual in Punjabi and English. They had already begun working in a local mosque with a group of children whose parents were concerned about their progress in school. They decided to apply for a small grant to see if they could further develop their ideas on a bilingual approach to teaching and learning. When this was successful, they held a well-attended family meeting where they explained their hopes and ideas to a large group of interested parents and other relatives from a range of language, cultural and social backgrounds. They launched complementary Saturday classes in a local primary school, where virtually all pupils were bilingual. Fortunately, the school had a sympathetic headteacher who had already done much to promote community links, and teachers who also showed interest. The classes were not just for the children in the school, but were open to the whole community. Because a significant number of families in the area were of Bangladeshi heritage, Saiqa and Reefath invited a third teacher, Shila Begum, to join them. Shila had recently completed her teacher training, with a specialism in Early Years, and was keen to participate.

All three teachers are of second-generation South Asian heritage, brought up 'living in two or more languages' (Hall, 2001) as members of large extended family networks that maintain strong links with their heritage countries. They were all educated in schools in Bradford and completed their teacher training in the local college. They and their families experienced in their lives on a daily basis the effects of national and local education policies in the 1980s and 1990s. These included the separation of community language classes from mainstream schooling recommended by the Swann Report (DES, 1985), and the introduction of the monolingual and 'monolingualising' (Heller, 1995) National Curriculum in 1988. As student teachers, they learned how to use the National Literacy Strategy, developing skills in teaching children to read at word, sentence and text level. They have all experienced the professional benefits of bilingualism in their personal lives, and the ways it can be used as a positive tool for learning in mainstream classrooms. They have also had powerful personal experiences of their bilingualism being unrecognised and devalued in mainstream classrooms. Saiqa and Reefath were involved in the Primary National Strategy pilot project for children with English as an Additional Language. Shila has worked in a mainstream school to promote bilingual approaches with new arrivals, mostly from countries in the expanded EU. They see their ability to promote children's learning bilingually as a resource (Conteh, 2007a) and a positive aspect of their identities as primary teachers (Conteh, 2007b). Their commitment to bilingual learning and teaching is personal as well as professional.

The BLTA classes

The bilingual Saturday classes have been running since 2002. They are for children aged 5-11 and are free of charge, being funded by a series of small grants from Education Bradford and voluntary bodies. The host school has a very positive attitude to the ideas promoted by the BLTA, and provides rent-free accommodation and a base for meetings and to store resources. Normally, around twenty children from a roll of about 30 attend from 9.00-12.00 every Saturday. Their parents are encouraged to stay but usually do not as they have many family commitments and chores to carry out. The teachers have run a short series of workshops for parents where they encouraged them to work with their children employing the strategies they used in the classes. These were successful in helping the parents to understand how they could work with their children at home.

The main goal of the classes is to develop and enhance children's understanding of and confidence in using their mother tongue to help support their learning in mainstream schools. The children are usually organised into two groups, one for older and one for younger children. For part of the time, everyone will be together, and at times the children work in mixed age groups. Work is planned round a theme and often uses story-based activities. The teachers use a lot of Maths and Literacy games to develop the children's skills in these parts of the mainstream curriculum. The teachers also take opportunities to extend the children's experience of language diversity and the wider world, as when a group of MA students were invited to visit from the University of York. The resulting sharing of language knowledge was a powerful learning experience for all involved (Conteh, 2007c).

Shila Begum describes her work at the BLTA

I mainly work with children who are either in Reception, Year One or Year Two (ages 5-7) so there is a wide range of abilities and ages. Therefore I adopt creative teaching methods to gain the children's curiosity and enthusiasm. I often use a range of visual stimuli to help contextualise activities. I believe in child-initiated learning, so when children show an interest in a particular area, I pursue this further. An example of this was when the children learnt about the baobab tree. This took place in the course of four sessions. I worked with a group of ten children; two Bengali speaking children, two Arabic speaking children and six Punjabi/Urdu speaking children.

Session One – A Strange Tree

On this occasion, I started the activity not knowing what to expect. I hoped I would be able to encourage a lot of talk from the children. I chose to show them a video of a Bangla song. The song was about Bangladesh and was called *Ami Banglar Gaan Ghai* (I sing the song of Bangladesh). My aim was for the children to observe the different scenery of Bangladesh during different seasons and comment on the bright sunny colourful atmosphere and the lush green paddy fields that turn gold during the harvest season. The children watched the video intensely and with great concentration. They described the colours as I had hoped and hummed along with the song. As the song played on, it reached the point where the singer sat in front of a very large tree. At once the children looked surprised and commented on the vast size of the tree and its strange shape. They all wanted to know what the tree was called, but unfortunately at the time I had no idea. The following week Jean came to visit us at the Saturday classes so we asked her if she knew the name of the tree. She informed us that it was a baobab tree. I later asked my parents if they knew what the Bengali name for this tree was, and they replied '*Bot gaas*'.

Session Two – The Baobab Tree

Jean gave us a book about the baobab tree and we looked at the pictures and learnt more about the tree. I asked the children to describe the tree in their own words. Below are some of the responses I collected:

'The baobab tree looks crunchy and the flowers fell off.' (Maria, aged 6)

'The leaves fell off it looked crunchy.' (Faris, aged 5)

'When you touch it, it feels like an elephant's foot.' (Elmontaser, aged 7)

'The baobab looked scary.' (Alifiyah, aged 4)

One child described the baobab tree in Bengali, '*Bot gaas boro ar suka ar ulta, ami gaas bala fai, ami bangladesho gele gaas dekhmu.*' (The baobab tree is big and pointy and upside down and I like it, when I go to Bangladesh I will see the tree.) (Saleh, aged 5)

Session Three – The Baobab Tree Myth

Once the children had discussed the baobab tree we discovered that there was an African myth explaining how it was created. We explored this further and found that long ago there lived a great spirit who summoned all the animals in the world to plant a tree. Each animal came and chose a tree to plant except for a lazy hyena who arrived late and was given the very last tree. He was in such a hurry that he planted the tree upside down. That is why the baobab tree looks as if it is growing upside down and the branches look like roots growing out of the ground. The children retold the myth about the baobab tree orally in pairs and in small groups and practised telling their stories in English and in their mother tongue. This is how Farah retold the myth:

> There were some animals and they were picking some trees up and the last animal had the smallest tree and it was a baobab tree. The baobab tree is old and bumpy. So he decided to go and plant it far away and he didn't know, so he planted it upside down. (Farah, aged 6)

Session Four – Baobab Tree Pictures

I believe that children like to express themselves through the medium of art, therefore I encouraged the group of children to draw pictures of the baobab tree and images from the video they had seen, using different art media such as collage, chalk drawing and pencil crayons. Once their pictures were completed I asked them to describe what they had drawn. I then went on to compile a small booklet containing all their pictures and statements to celebrate their achievements.

Singing in Punjabi

We then talked about children's own beliefs about how things were created. All the children in the group were Muslim and they replied that Allah had created everything. So we decided to sing a song in Punjabi titled *Kisne banaiya puloko?* (Who made the flowers?). The next line goes on to say '*Wo jo upar rehta hai*' (The one who lives high above – Allah). All of the children enjoyed singing this song in Punjabi, including those whose mother tongue was not Punjabi.

Some general thoughts

These activities encouraged the children to use their bilingual skills freely by giving them the opportunity to work in a more informal context than the mainstream classroom. Also, because the activities were creative and fun, children became immersed in them and were able to get fully involved as there were many ideas to talk about. They were buzzing with curiosity and displayed a natural desire to want to learn about the baobab tree. They enjoyed expressing the ideas through their drawings and also used their bilingual skills enthusiastically.

An example of how different languages can support one another in learning came from another activity when 8-year-old Kieran described how she counted in fives. After she had been taught to count in fives in Urdu at the BLTA class she used this method for herself in school. She explained that it was much easier to calculate the sums in Urdu and then convert the answers into English. Kieran stated that this was how she preferred to do her numeracy work in mainstream school. Similarly, many parents have informed me that after attending BLTA classes, their child's confidence has increased considerably and their teachers have noticed a change in them.

I am proud to be part of the BLTA and thoroughly enjoy teaching and exploring innovative methods of working with bilingual children.

Bradford's Policy on Multilingualism: Principles
Education Bradford

English is the primary language of education and communication in this country. Therefore all children have a right to effective teaching of English and in English.

Support in all the languages in a child's repertoire helps to ensure that children have the best access to new concepts and ideas and therefore to the highest possible achievement. It is essential that this starts with a strong foundation in the early years and continues as children grow older.

Language is a fundamental aspect of identity. Acknowledging and promoting children's ability to communicate in their home languages builds self confidence and encourages pupils' belief in themselves as learners.

Access to a range of languages increases social and community cohesion and is an entitlement for all pupils. An ability to communicate in more than one language is a social and life advantage.

Promoting home languages at school and within the school's community, including communicating with parents in ways which are accessible to them, builds community links and mutual respect. This encourages families and schools to work in partnership to develop children's full range of language competencies.

Awareness of the systems and structures of one language aids the learning of other languages.

Achievement in more than one language develops the capacity to enjoy being a confident and competent user of spoken and written language for an expanding range of purposes.

The approach to language development is inclusive and values the language heritages and experiences of all pupils and adults within the educational community.

Education Bradford (2004)

Turkish community action in the Netherlands: Campaigning to retain mother tongue education
Kutlay Yagmur, Tilburg University

C lasses in children's home languages used to be provided in the Netherlands during the primary school day. But recently, as in other European countries, including Denmark and Norway, such classes have been abolished. It seems that home languages are no longer admissible in the classroom – and some policy makers and politicians do not want these languages to be heard in school playgrounds either. The leader of a right-wing party in Denmark even proposed a ban on immigrant languages in the home, arguing that speaking languages other than Danish would block children's social and linguistic integration. In answer to such political moves, immigrant groups have developed their own strategies and solutions. In the Netherlands, this struggle has highlighted two important issues: that language policy often flies in the face of research, and that communities can resist policy changes by responding with their own initiatives.

Policies based on language ideologies
Dutch policy makers used three arguments for abolishing mother tongue classes, none of which are justifiable according to current research. Instead, they reveal underlying negative ideologies concerning minority languages.

Argument A
'Home language instruction acts as a barrier to the integration of immigrant children'
This argument is only put forward with respect to immigrant minority languages. Learning English, for instance, is not considered to obstruct the social integration of English speaking children growing up in the Netherlands, and the learning of English is supported even in kindergarten. But where an immigrant language is concerned, policy makers display political resistance.

Argument B
'No scientific evidence is available to prove that a good basis in the first language leads to a strong basis in second language acquisition'
Policy makers are still using so-called scientific evidence from the 1960s. As reviewed in detail by Baker (2006), such arguments are old-fashioned and basically ideological in nature. Recent research, using more reliable methodology, has shown that well-grounded concept development in the first language has positive effects on the second language. The bilingualism literature

110

is full of evidence in support of additive bilingual instruction but in an anti-immigrant era, there is no political support for these languages.

Argument C

'*Home language instruction was done very poorly anyway – the teachers mostly did not have appropriate teaching qualifications*'

If this were actually the case, the solution would not lie in stopping instruction but in improving the quality of teacher training programmes, providing appropriate pedagogic materials and increasing the status of these languages by making them part of the regular curriculum in schools. Instead, the classes were abolished, leaving 60,000 Turkish children deprived of maintaining their heritage language.

Community resistance to language policy

Creating a language policy does not guarantee its successful implementation. As pointed out by Lewis (1981:262)

> Any policy for language, especially in the system of education, has to take account of the attitudes of those likely to be affected. In the long run, no policy will succeed which does not do one of three things: conform to the expressed attitudes of those involved; persuade those who express negative attitudes about the rightness of the policy; or seek to remove the causes of the disagreement. In any case, knowledge about attitudes is fundamental to the formulation of a policy as well as to success in its implementation.

Turkish community action in the Netherlands has proved the accuracy of Lewis's proposition. Turkish immigrants displayed a strong reaction against the new policy. A number of organisations issued declarations against the abolition of mother tongue classes. In several cities, Turkish mothers organised protests and submitted thousands of signatures calling for withdrawal of the policy. All these protests showed that Dutch policy makers had made their decision without any consideration of the attitudes of the parents. Turkish mothers demanded Turkish instruction from the local schools, but their efforts were fruitless. Drawing on political backing from the post-September 11 anti-immigrant backlash in mainstream society, the policy makers reiterated their rejection of home language instruction in schools. By sacking 1,400 mother tongue teachers, they gave a strong message that an irreversible process had started. Yet, as Lewis (1981) stated, the success of a policy is not one-sided. If one of the parties does not recognise the legitimacy of the act, then implementation is difficult.

After the abolition of home language instruction, minority language communities began their own initiatives, both at national and local level, to maintain instruction for primary school children in an extra-curricular and complementary manner. The Arab community started organising mother tongue classes in the local mosques. A number of Turkish religious organisations opted for the same strategy. However, realising this could lead to community language instruction becoming marginalised outside mainstream education, Turkish academics working at different Dutch universities formulated an alternative language policy. This had five successive stages:

- Preparation and mobilisation
- Dissemination and awareness raising
- Organising instruction based at local schools
- Resuming instruction
- Inspection

Preparation and mobilisation

The first stage aimed at mobilising Turkish community members against the abolition of mother tongue teaching. An internet site was set up to inform parents, with the slogan *Türkce icin el ele* (Hand-in-hand for Turkish, www. turkce-icin-el-ele.nl), and in a very short period of time around 10,000 people registered their support for Turkish education. National and local media showed extensive interest, with coverage almost every day in Turkish-language newspapers. Having successfully completed the first stage, the Turkish-Dutch Education Foundation (Stichting TON) was established to gain an institutional identity.

Dissemination and awareness raising

The goal of the second stage was to raise further awareness of the importance of Turkish instruction. Within six months about 40 meetings were organised in towns and cities with a significant Turkish population. Turkish parents, mostly mothers, attended these meetings in large numbers. They heard lectures on the aims of the community action, as well as information concerning the importance of mother tongue instruction for the cognitive and emotional development of children. These meetings were extremely valuable because they revealed that most parents had been persuaded not to speak in mother tongue to their children. Some mainstream schools had provided inaccurate information suggesting that if parents spoke in Turkish, children would not learn Dutch fully and would be disadvantaged in school. The second stage was therefore crucial for providing parents with accurate information in

Hollanda'da Türkçe dersi başlıyor

Türkçe Bayramı

Hollanda hükümetinin uyumu engellediği gerekçesiyle parasal desteği kesmesi sonucu ilkokullarda geçtiğimiz ağustos ayından bu yana verilemeyen Türkçe dersleri, velilerin çığ gibi büyüyen sivil toplum hareketiyle tekrar başladı

9. Newspaper coverage of the campaign to retain Turkish classes

order to gain their support for Turkish classes. Parents were told that Turkish education needed to take place in schools rather than in mosques or community organisations.

Organising school-based instruction

After each meeting, a number of volunteers were nominated as the local representatives of the Turkish-Dutch Education Foundation, and given the responsibility of setting up Turkish classes. Their first task was to register all Turkish-speaking children aged 6 to 12. They then contacted the local school management and asked for classes to conduct teaching in extra-curricular hours. Some schools opened their doors wholeheartedly, but others demanded a huge rent for each class. In the municipality of Eindhoven for instance, the Board of Managers for Schools demanded 16 euros per hour per class, which meant paying around 40,000 euros per year. Such an enormous charge would prevent the establishment of Turkish classes in that city, so parents wrote protest letters to the Ministry of Education. The Minister, Maria van der Hoeven, sent a letter to all schools stating that they could not charge more than 5 euros rent per hour, but some local boards completely ignored this. Some school boards even suggested to parents that they should conduct Turkish instruction in local mosques instead. However, most schools cooperated with the Foundation and provided appropriate classrooms. Even though some religious Turkish organisations were prepared to offer places free of charge, the Foundation insisted that education needed to take place in children's mainstream schools. This goal has mostly been achieved.

Resuming instruction

Teachers have been selected by a commission of parents and educational specialists from the Foundation, in accordance with rules and conditions used by the Dutch Ministry of Education. The teachers are hired by the Foundation and paid through parental contributions. Turkish instruction has now resumed in schools, monitored by a group of local representatives. Because instruction takes place after school hours, two mothers are responsible for assisting the teachers in each school.

Inspection

In the final stage, teachers are inspected by educational specialists from the Foundation. Bi-monthly seminars are organised to provide in-service training and promote increased interaction amongst teachers. Any teachers who could not fulfill the demands of the Foundation or who could not work in close co-operation with schools have been re-trained for better performance. This close cooperation between parents, teachers and the Foundation's specialists has improved the teaching-learning process and student numbers have increased.

Results of community action

Within a very short time, the Foundation has acquired more than 40,000 members and now offers Turkish instruction for primary school children in over twenty municipalities across the country. At the moment, 3,500 children receive Turkish instruction in the schools they attend. The Foundation is successful in small cities where the parents are easy to mobilise. However, in large cities such as Rotterdam and Amsterdam schools do not cooperate and Turkish instruction is provided by a number of local marginal groups. The Turkish Education Foundation tries to find common ground for Turkish instruction in schools but political resistance is hard to overcome.

This bottom-up push for instruction in Turkish has not found any political resistance in the Ministry of Education. The Minister herself expressed support for the activities of the Foundation. Yet she admitted that the Ministry could not provide any financial support at present due to the negative political climate in mainstream society.

The Foundation has multiple goals. As well as providing instruction in Turkish, the ultimate goal is pressurising policy makers for new legislation in which Turkish becomes part of the regular curriculum. Political lobbying and campaigns are planned to achieve this purpose. The Foundation aims to keep the matter of mother tongue teaching on the agenda of both parents and schools. If this important issue loses its priority for parents, the struggle will be a lost cause. Because the Board of the Foundation is aware of this social reality, they aim to maintain the campaigning spirit through regular meetings.

Lessons to be learned

Turkish community action in the Netherlands has shown that if one of the parties does not accept the imposed language policy, a revision of the policy can be achieved. It has also shown that as well as official policy implemented by the government, there can be group-based policies to protect community interests. Because Turkish language is one of the most esteemed core values of Turkish identity, fear of losing their mother tongue in the context of immigration has mobilised Turkish people to set up their own language classes in the Netherlands. The reaction of Dutch policy makers is rather cautious at the moment, perhaps presuming that without financial resources and active guidance the Foundation cannot maintain these classes. The Turkish Education Foundation can always ask for financial support from the homeland, but the current Board of Directors prefers self-sustaining solutions. Because the majority of Turkish immigrants hold Dutch citizenship, the Foundation considers they are entitled to claim support from their own government in the Netherlands.

Finally – and importantly – the case of Turkish in the Netherlands demonstrates how the need to campaign actively for home language instruction can generate a new level of awareness and understanding of bilingualism among minority communities.

Learning connections

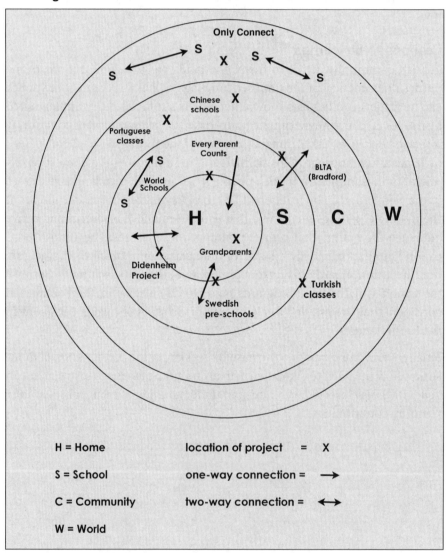

Thanks to Gildas Bernier

116

Conclusion to Part 2

Reflecting on the contributions in Part 2, we note that the first and most crucial step in creating learning communities is for schools to understand that learning can be informal as well as formal, taking place in home and community settings as well as at school. This not only means school practices being transported into the home, but also means giving recognition to different kinds of learning experiences – in terms of content, strategies and relationships – that occur outside the mainstream classroom. Once this recognition takes place, schools, together with families and community organisations, can begin to explore ways of linking with children's out-of-school learning,.

The diagram opposite shows different spaces in which learning takes place: home, school, community and the wider world. Connections can be built within and across these spaces: for example between home and school, school and school, or school and community. The diagram locates each of the initiatives discussed in Part 2 within a particular space, or at the border of two spaces that are becoming interconnected. The arrows show connections currently taking place, and the direction of the flow of knowledge.

Sometimes the interconnections are yet to be made, such as between schools and grandparents, whose knowledge tends to remain within the home context, or between Portuguese and Chinese community-run classes and mainstream schools, since learning in the community is often invisible in the mainstream. Turkish classes in the Netherlands are poised on the border between community and school, as mainstream schools have yet to understand the full value of the language learning taking place on their premises. In other cases connections have been made, but are only one-way at present, such as for the Every Parent Counts project, which gives parents a window on school education but does not yet aim to bring ideas from home into school. However, power relations can change in the relationships between and across

117

spaces, as with home-school links through work in Didenheim, Stockholm and Bradford, and links between local schools in Utrecht, or schools around Europe in the Only Connect project. Intercultural issues come to the fore through this contact, requiring negotiation and dialogue around different ideas and practices. The result can be learning communities that are continually revitalised through a process of dynamic exchange.

Part 3
Learners, teachers and schools

Section editors:
Tina Hickey and Dominique Portante

Overview of Part 3

The concluding section of the book looks at institutional aspects of language learning in multilingual contexts, surveying national and pan-European policies on language learning, teacher education to prepare for linguistically diverse school populations, and differing language learning situations where a variety of approaches are taken to develop children's plurilingual capacities.

We begin with learners because, in an ideal world, learners would drive systems. Language learning pedagogies cover a continuum, from learning a language as a single subject, through learning some content through the language, to total immersion in the target language. Different situations generate a thought-provoking range of possibilities, and there is an added value in examining the application of particular pedagogies in the context of minority languages. Rather than seeing these pedagogies as tools that can be implemented neutrally, it is inevitable that their operation will be affected by the power relationships within which they are put into practice. For example, we need to recognise that even young children become aware of the lower status accorded to their minority language (Hickey, 2007; Kenner *et al*, 2008), and therefore we need to remain continually alert to the socio-political dimensions within which multilingual education operates.

What is needed is ongoing revision and evaluation by reflective practitioners and other researchers, so that we empower children by helping them to 'read the world' as well as 'read the word,' to use Freire and Macedo's (1987) terms. A 'pedagogy of possibility' (*ibid*:60) enables learners to draw on their existing knowledge, so that they can 'appropriate their own discourses and simultaneously move beyond them' (*ibid*:54). Without such a pedagogy, school language and literacy programmes merely give children access to 'a pre-established discourse silencing their own voices' (Freire and Macedo, 1987: 55-56). This is the case when educational practices and policies are conceived within an assimilative perspective, where adaptation to the mainstream culture is the only priority and where maintenance of minority languages is considered unnecessary. Teachers concerned with inclusive practices need to distance themselves from the dominant context and construct a broader picture that liberates children from constraints by legitimising the uses of all languages in the classroom. New learning spaces can then be shaped by the children's plurilingual discourses, promoting language and literacy as tools for cultural development.

Pedagogies of possibility could also include approaches such as 'translanguaging' (Williams, 2000; Baker, 2006), where the input to pupils is in one of their languages and output tasks require them to use another language, drawing on their multilingual resources, including codeswitching. This offers children an opportunity to take on a variety of roles in authentic communicative contexts. Cummins (2008) notes that research now points to the improved learning opportunities that bilingual instructional strategies such as translanguaging provide, particularly for children from minority language backgrounds. As well as being important for cognitive development, using mother tongue in learning supports children's identity construction as participants in different cultural communities, thus developing 'multimembership' in the sense discussed by Wenger (1998).

What kinds of policies would promote such pedagogies of possibility? It must be recognised that policies tend to be developed at the macro level, without necessarily being democratically representative. The ideal would be a framework that brings together the insights of researchers, practitioners and policy makers. This would re-allocate power, seeing policies as dynamic and evolving in the course of their implementation by practitioners at the micro level, with adjustments to local needs and resources, and requiring critical analysis.

Another area of possibility in both policy and pedagogy is opened up by the shift from the predominantly instrumental view of motivation to learn language which was inherent in earlier EU language policy documents, with goals such as competitiveness and mobility, to the more recent recognition of the value of integrative motivation, involving openness to other viewpoints and cultures (Dörnyei, 2001). This shift is highly significant, and points to a re-evaluation of languages as offering a personally enriching resource, rather than merely serving basic communication and employment functions. Closely allied to this is a growing recognition in language policies that all languages are valuable, including minority and migrant languages. The realisation that language learning is a lifelong right for all citizens, and should not be restricted to the small set of languages formerly recognised as having value, but include all languages of significance for individual learners, constitutes a fundamental change of view, and offers a 'policy of possibility'. Translating such policy into effective practice presents a demanding but immensely rewarding challenge for educators and policy makers in the future.

6
Learners in different contexts

This chapter considers how locally constructed pedagogies can build spaces for multilingualism in different sociopolitical contexts. In Luxembourg, although the curriculum is trilingual in Luxembourgish, French and German, children from other linguistic backgrounds do not generally have opportunities to use their languages at school. However, some teachers in pre-schools and primary schools have developed innovative practices that foster plurilingual learning spaces. An example from Israel, where two communities are in political conflict, shows how bilingual schools can work to counter the politics of separation by creating spaces of co-existence for Hebrew and Arabic speakers. In Ireland, Irish immersion pre-schools provide a space officially dedicated to the development of a threatened indigenous language, but steps need to be taken to ensure that this space is used for the benefit of L1 minority speakers as well as new (L2) speakers of Irish. A Spanish-English nursery in South London also works to foster bilingualism in an English-dominant context, and an innovative school in Eastern England promotes an international dimension to enhance learning and aid social inclusion in a multilingual and multicultural society.

Plurilingualism and plurilingual literacy among young learners in Luxembourg
Dominique Portante and Charles Max,
University of Luxembourg

In Luxembourg, the diversity of children's linguistic backgrounds presents all the actors in school with a major challenge: how the learning of language and literacy can take place in a plurilingual context. A research project on children's plurilingualism (Portante *et al*, 2007) revealed a range of tensions that arise when the complex linguistic backgrounds of the children clash with normative, curriculum-oriented and teacher-centred instructional practices relying on prescribed textbooks and pre-structured activities. Nevertheless, these underlying tensions encourage teachers to transform their classroom practices to create innovative plurilingual classroom spaces that address the needs of a changing population. Research data reveal that the children's linguistic and culturally diverse backgrounds work as resources for learning as they expand opportunities for participation and for the learning of all children.

We begin this chapter with a brief description of the educational context in Luxembourg and children's use of languages. Two videotaped excerpts from our research data enable us to spotlight how language and literacy learning in pre-school and primary classrooms is shaped by, and shapes, the material, social and historical dimensions of the learning context. We end by emphasising future prospects for developing classroom practices in the domains of language and literacy.

Educational context and children's use of languages

One of the most striking points about language use in Luxembourg is the country's institutional trilingualism in Luxembourgish, French and German. This trilingualism developed historically, was recognised statewide by law in 1984, and is put into practice in school for all children (Horner and Weber, 2008). At pre-school level the curriculum language is *Lëtzebuergesch*, a Germanic, Moselle Franconian variety, which is the national language. In primary school, German is used as the language for reading and writing in first grade. German becomes progressively the main curriculum language as children move through primary school, while French is taught as a subject from Grade Two onwards and Luxembourgish is used in subjects such as arts and crafts, for musical and physical education, and for communicating in informal contexts.

124

10. School sign in Luxembourgish

While around 60% of the school population are Luxembourgish citizens by law, language use within families shows a far more complex picture. A recent national survey focusing on the languages that 3 to 9-year-old children use when interacting at home found that *Lëtzebuergesch* is the most frequently used language in 51% of family contexts, Portuguese in 19% and French in 14%. Other languages present significantly lower percentages: 3% or less (Maurer *et al*, 2007) .

However, the survey also revealed the linguistic complexity of the home contexts in which the large majority of children live. Most are exposed to two or more languages, and there are some interesting findings about the three officially recognised languages of the country. In contexts outside the family, most children use *Lëtzebuergesch* with their peers. In their home settings, many siblings of Portuguese origin also interact in *Lëtzebuergesch* or French. A minority of Luxembourgish parents use French with their children, and Luxembourgish children come into contact with German early through the use of audio-visual and print media.

Our theoretical framework

For our analysis, we developed a comprehensive framework to study the intertwined learning of languages and literacy in this setting. Literacy is understood as a social practice situated within particular contexts and shaped by social interaction. According to Barton and Hamilton's approach, 'literacy is primarily something people do; it is an activity, located in the space between thought and text' (1998:3). In addition, we look at learning and development from a socio-cultural perspective, paying particular attention to the cultural resources that mediate an individual's participation and engagement in the activities of a community.

Context is a particularly important notion within our framework, since we aim to analyse how the social, material and historical dimensions of an activity are woven together to form a meaningful context for learning (Cole, 1996). In order to understand how literacy practices are shaped by and shape specific contexts, we draw on cultural-historical activity theory (CHAT) in line with Engeström's work (Engeström *et al*, 1999). CHAT emphasises the productive role of tensions and contradictions that arise within and between activity systems, such as home, school, and everyday contexts. An activity theory analysis also provides a productive starting point from which to consider how to reorganise the activity of a given context and create extended opportunities for innovation and change.

126

Following Razfar and Gutiérrez (2003), the construction of meaning provides the basis for literacy practices and 'is always situated and embedded within human activity systems that are goal directed and rule governed' (p39). Finally, we also refer to the Bakhtinian concept of 'multivoicedness' (Bakhtin, 1981:293-294) in order to highlight our perception of diversity as a resource for enriching meaning.

Within this framework, we define literacy practices as the cultural ways in which individuals use written language as a tool for transforming themselves and their contexts. In addition, we place a particular emphasis on the hybrid and broader semiotic resources of interconnected communities such as home, pre-school and primary school, including processes and movements taking place at and across their boundaries.

Overcoming tensions between the children's contexts and school practices

Our research on children's plurilingualism in Luxembourg highlighted how children and teachers deal differently with the challenge of using cultural and linguistic diversity as a resource for learning languages and literacy (Portante *et al*, 2007). Here we briefly discuss two classroom activities videotaped at a primary school with Portuguese children, who form a significant part of the immigrant population in Luxembourg (Max *et al*, 2005).

The first example, from a French lesson in a third grade classroom, reveals processes related to a writing activity. The task was to produce a self-portrait according to the pre-defined templates of the official textbook. Classroom interaction was ruled by teacher-led IRF (input-response-feedback) formats, leaving little space for the children's home languages, voices and meanings. Like many Portuguese children in Luxembourg, David, a 10-year-old boy, speaks Portuguese at home, is quite fluent in vernacular French, which he uses with his older siblings, and learned Luxembourgish and also German within the formal setting of school.

In this task, David was asked to present a self-portrait in words. He started filling in some information about himself, using the given patterns from the textbook. When asked to read his French composition aloud to the whole class, he performed poorly, giving the impression of a child who struggles with French and finds it difficult to form sentences. However, David's involvement with the learning activity became quite different after the lesson, when he presented his work to the researcher. In this interaction, when he was free from completing the pre-defined classroom task, he was able to demonstrate his lived experience. The result was that his discourse gained an entirely different quality, becoming more fluent and rich, as he introduced new personal information, such as his experience of having a pet at home. Combining his vernacular French resources with the school's standard French, his production became part of the intertextual chain of discourses, texts and meanings relevant to him. When he could not find the right French words, he used Luxembourgish to convey his meaning.

Thus, the personal dimension only became evident in David's output when the learning context changed and gave him the opportunity to bring his own social experiences, interests and cultural resources into play.

Our second example is in sharp contrast to the more traditional view of language learning as the acquisition of a set of skills that we observed in David's third grade classroom, where the children's voices, meanings and former linguistic experiences existed, but solely outside the official space for literacy learning. Here a group of teachers from pre-school and first grade collaborated to enact continuity in their language and literacy related classroom practices, to bridge the gap between both school settings. They jointly devised novel learning practices to tackle the challenging task of learning a new language and becoming literate in this language. In practical terms, they replaced the set textbook with the children's own books and set up sequences of activities that involved the children in various ways in language and literacy learning. When working in small groups on the children's books, the teachers and the children succeeded in creating innovative practices that permitted joint productive activity through the interplay of classroom and home voices, involving co-construction of shared meaning and peer to peer translation. New meanings of words were explored in the different languages of the children, using the children's home languages for scaffolding purposes and to enhance participation.

The fact that the groups were mixed, or 'hybrid', was the key to the joint language production. The teachers chose to work with mixed groups of children who brought different levels of familiarity with activity formats, and different levels of competence in *Lëtzebuergesch*, German and various home languages into the activity. They consciously drew upon the children's varied resources and turned them into tools for learning by combining them with the semiotic tools of the classroom.

A new rule was introduced legitimising children's use of their home languages. Plurilingual speech and non-verbal forms of communication became valid forms of participation in the learning community. Although the teachers regulated the activity, they were prepared to hand over control to the children who were considered experts in their own languages. The roles of experts and novices were not fixed but were continuously negotiated. Translation was clearly marked as an additional expertise.

Thus these pre-school and first grade teachers expanded the object of the learning activity beyond classroom borders, by interconnecting social and linguistic spaces through shared tools (books), jointly defined rules, flexible negotiation of roles and deliberately mixed learning groups. In so doing, they overcame the tension between the children's contexts and the practices legitimated by the school.

Promising outlooks for language and literacy learning

In our research, continuity in children's strategies across contexts facilitates productive literacy practices. This continuity occurs when children:

- have rich opportunities to draw on their experiences across boundaries
- get involved in joint activities where they can take initiatives and share their thoughts and ideas, drawing on their cultural resources to develop understanding of the world and working with familiar tools from everyday contexts like their own books
- feel that their productions are valued as part of the intertextual chain of discourses and meanings relevant to them

Continuity in teaching strategies is also of major concern. Successful practices can be characterised according to the following four dimensions:

Drawing on semiotic resources across boundaries

School and home languages are integrated to make sense of the activity and to build up the new languages: *Lëtzebuergesch* in pre-school, German and French in primary school.

Organising hybrid literacy practices

The broad semiotic resources of plurilingual groups are deliberately used to facilitate meaning making and understanding. Children are encouraged to become aware of the various cultural resources available to them, their own competence, their identities and the specific context within which they are working.

Creating joint productive activity

Joint productive activity increases communication and mutual assistance, with the teacher as one resource amongst others. The CHAT framework emphasises the role of the activity itself. The members of the learning community constantly create outcomes through collaborative actions that broaden the range of available tools for the activity, thus creating new opportunities for participation.

Fostering literacy as a tool for development

Learning environments at pre-school and primary school draw continuously on the cultural tools provided by literacy and language. These tools mediate children's construction of knowledge about the world. They also enhance children's processes of self-reflection, self-regulation and awareness of their own thinking.

To conclude, we argue that innovative practices such as using the children's home languages need to be legitimated by official policy and by teachers. This is an important starting-point for teachers who consciously aim to draw on the potential of diversity. The pre-school and first grade teachers show us the way by linking language activities to former and current meanings in children's lives, thus creating contexts for joint development.

Bilingualism and biliteracy as the norm: Arabic/Hebrew bilingual schools in Israel from a socio-political perspective

Aura Mor-Sommerfeld, University of Haifa

Historical developments have created a unique and complicated situation in the state of Israel, founded in 1948. Two populations with two different languages live in conflict in the same state. The Israelis speak Hebrew, even though this is not necessarily their mother tongue, while the Arab-Palestinian population's mother tongue is Arabic, though almost all of them also speak Hebrew. The foundation of the Israeli state thus created a paradoxical situation in regard to language: Hebrew is the language of the Israeli majority, but it is a minority language in the Middle East, while Arabic, the language of Israel's minority population, is a majority language in the Middle East. Added to this situation is the presence of a number of other groups with different mother tongues who have migrated to Israel.

Hebrew and Arabic speakers in Israel live separately and yet interact daily. There are separate cities, small towns and villages for each community. Only a few cities have both populations and even those have separate neighbourhoods and community life, including separate schools. Yet these two populations interface in some areas, such as at work, or in public institutions including hospitals, government offices, football stadiums and universities. However, most Hebrew speakers rarely encounter Arabic speakers, and tend not to see Arabic as having value for internal and international communication needs. This is coloured by the ongoing conflict between Israelis and Palestinians which affects daily life, including the educational system. The most dramatic events, the expulsion of 700,000 Palestinians during the 1948 War (called the War of Independence by Israeli Jews, and the *Nakbeh* – the disaster – by Arab-Palestinians) and the demolition of more than 400 of their villages, have created a hostile relationship between the two nations (Mor-Sommerfeld *et al*, 2007). This is the core of the majority-minority relationship, and is highly relevant to education in Israel.

The education system in Israel

The education system in Israel is mainly public, and most of its schools are run by the Ministry of Education, under whose control and supervision there are two separate systems: one for Jewish Israelis, Hebrew speakers, the other for Palestinian citizens, Arabic speakers. This means that Palestinian citizens of Israel and Jewish schoolchildren are educated in separate schools, each with its own culture, religion and linguistic heritage. Obviously, this separation also applies to teachers, parents and the school staff, and affects teacher-training courses in colleges. However, although segregation according to identities dominates education, borders are sometimes crossed, and this division is not absolutely rigid.

Educational policies and curricula derive from a socio-political reality; and in Israel, this means that in both the Hebrew and Arabic schools, they derive from the Zionist origins of the State of Israel. School curricula are always in Hebrew for Hebrew schools and Arabic for Arab schools. In some subjects they differ in content (eg literature, religion, tradition), while in others the programmes are quite similar (eg sciences, citizenship). The most marked difference is in the cultural and historical approaches (Al-Haj, 2002; Benavot and Resh, 2003). Hebrew speaking pupils receive extensive courses in Judaism and Jewish and Israeli history. Palestinian history and culture are not taught in Arab schools in Israel. There is also asymmetry in the allocation of teaching hours in the two streams for world history, Arab history and Jewish history. Al-Haj (2002) notes that, while Arabic speakers receive extensive schooling in Hebrew and regard Hebrew literature and tradition as part of their curriculum, Hebrew students have no programmes concerning Arabic literature or tradition in theirs. Exposure to Arab-Palestinian culture therefore only takes place at occasional events or through the enterprise of local school principals or supervisors (Mor-Sommerfeld *et al*, 2007). Regarding language study, all children with Arabic as L1 (first language) study Hebrew as L2 (second language) as part of their general curriculum, but the converse is not the case with Arabic for Hebrew L1 pupils. Naturally, such a policy influences the attitudes of children from both communities, not just concerning each other's language, but also regarding each other's beliefs, rights and emotions (Amara and Mari, 2002).

In this context a new, small-scale model of Arabic-Hebrew bilingual schooling has been developed, which aims to challenge the reality of segregation and hostility, and to offer an alternative approach to education and society.

Bilingual schools in Israel

There are now five bilingual Arabic-Hebrew schools operating in Israel: in Neve Shalom-Wahat alSalaam (Oasis of Peace, opened in 1984), the Galilee (opened in 1997), Jerusalem (1998), the Bridge across the Wadi School in Wadi Ara (2004) and Hagar School in Be'er Sheva (2007). The Neve Shalom-Wahat alSalaam school is located in the only mixed village in Israel, where Jews and Arabs live together in a *shared* community. All the schools were opened as private initiatives, usually by parents helped by non-governmental organisations (NGOs), for example 'Hand in Hand', 'The Bridge across the Wadi' and 'Hagar', and in cooperation with local municipalities. All are recognised by the Israeli Ministry of Education. Bilingual kindergartens operate in four of the schools (not in the Galilee) as a part of the educational framework. There are also two other bilingual kindergartens, one in Jerusalem (YMCA) and the other in Tivon, near Haifa.

In and around the model: political and critical issues

These schools are based more or less on the same model. The schools and kindergartens have approximately equal numbers of Arabic and Hebrew L1 children, and teachers *of* and *in* both languages, cultures and narratives. Thus, bilingual education in these schools is not just about languages, but also about other people's history and culture.

The bilingual education system uses a combination of two models, based on the two-way language immersion approach. This combination, proposed by

Mor-Sommerfeld (2005) and Amara (2005) has established a *cultural-cognitive model for bilingual education*, focusing on critical pedagogy (Freire, 1990) and critical literacy, and taking a socio-political perspective. According to this, the following elements and principles of bilingual pedagogy must be present in the bilingual school:

- approximately equal numbers of Arabic and Hebrew L1 pupils in each class
- two teachers – Arabic L1 and Hebrew L1 – sharing educational tasks, responsibilities and teaching for each class
- special training for teaching children in their first language
- both languages are taught and learnt together, without translation from one language to another
- children learn to read and write in both languages from the first day
- equal emphasis is placed on the narratives of both cultures
- literacy development in both languages is emphasised

During the early years in these schools, most lessons are taught by two teachers, each communicating in her/his first language. The socio-historical narrative of both populations is crucial to the school curriculum, and these are the only schools in Israel where both narratives are taught and learnt to the same extent. This is not just a matter of bridging between people and cultures or societies and languages, but of sharing and building a community based on common interests and mutual concerns.

11. Mural at bilingual school in Israel.

133

Language and literacy

Pedagogy in Israel's bilingual schools essentially adheres to the 'two-way' (Baker, 2006) and 'no translation' (Mor-Sommerfeld, 2005) models. The children entering school speak either Hebrew or Arabic. By the end of the first grade, most of them understand the second language, and almost all of them can read and write in both languages.

Learning two different scripts, though both of them are written from right to left, is one of the most fascinating aspects of the process. The children learn both written languages from the outset. Unlike developing a first language, children in the bilingual schools acquire writing in their L2 at the same time as speaking, and the written language thus acts as a lever activating the whole learning process. The children rely on the written language to develop the spoken one until they become fully bilingual. Language development is viewed as an integrated process, in which learners use their knowledge from L1 (eg of reading and writing, or of different genres) to develop their L2. At the same time, the learner can use ideas acquired during this process to create connections between the two languages, which also develops their mother tongue.

In the Israeli context, language must also be examined in terms of equality. Although conditions outside school are far from equal, the school environment is intended to be different. But nothing is simple. The fact is that Hebrew is much more in evidence. All the Arab teachers, parents and visitors speak Hebrew, whereas the opposite is rarely the case, so that the model of communication for children is that adults speak Hebrew but not necessarily Arabic. To achieve equal knowledge in both languages, more Arabic needs to be used. The curriculum is conducted in and between the two languages but Arabic and Hebrew are also subjects (both as L1 and L2) which are taught for 6-8 hours per week. English is taught and learned as a third language from third grade.

Language instruction and the role of teachers

Teaching in bilingual schools is a matter of choice, as is pupil enrolment. The teachers come from both communities and it is they who go through the most significant process of change (Mor-Sommerfeld, 2005). Most of them, especially the Hebrew teachers, have had no previous personal or professional relationships with teachers from the other culture, even though they all live in the same district. Furthermore, the Hebrew teachers do not usually speak Arabic, and have little knowledge about Arab culture and Palestinian history. Thus it is significant that the two teachers in each class share the teaching and responsibility for the children's needs. Each of them speaks in her/his mother tongue, working with all the children as their L1 or L2 teacher. They plan the study year together, prepare subject material and coordinate day-by-day instruction. Dialogue between the teachers is therefore ongoing.

However, Arabic L1 children do better in Hebrew L2 than Hebrew L1 children in Arabic L2. This parallels the general situation in Israel, where Arabic L1 speakers know Hebrew but Hebrew speakers do not know Arabic. The teachers' efforts to help children learn languages, and the status of the teachers themselves, are affected by the societal difference in language status. Bilingual schools in Israel are trying to realise their vision of a two-way languages model within a fragile framework in a challenging socio-political environment.

Towards a political perspective on bilingual education

The role of bilingual education in Israel is not just to promote language and cultural learning but also to bridge the gap between languages and communities. These schools must struggle not just to uphold a language curriculum, but also to change the reality of segregation. They must therefore be evaluated from a political perspective rather than only in terms of language knowledge.

Studies conducted in the schools in recent years (Feuerverger 2001; Bekerman and Shhadi, 2003; Amara, 2005; Mor-Sommerfeld, 2005) indicate that there is a great deal of willingness to deal with the Israeli-Palestinian conflict and to study and discuss both the Palestinian and Israeli narratives. At the same time, although the schools present an alternative, shared way of living and studying, they do not seem to engage with the national conflict in terms of political pedagogy or to challenge the communities around them. They too remain within their own boundaries and discourses. Bilingual schools need to work not just for themselves but as social agents with a comprehensive political perspective.

A bilingual society can never be fully democratic if it separates communities and their languages. It is to the society's own benefit to change matters, and it is the role and duty of the educational system to motivate and effect such a change. Although each bilingual community has unique characteristics, this model from Israel can be applied wherever two or more populations of different languages live together, whether or not they are in conflict. Bilingual education can be more than a means of teaching two languages: it can be a bridge between two communities.

The Anglo-Spanish Nursery School:
A Spanish/English bilingual programme
for children in South London
Gloria Gómez, Anglo-Spanish Nursery School

The Anglo-Spanish Nursery is a bilingual nursery school in Lambeth, South London, an area where 170 languages are spoken. It was set up in 1998 and caters for children from the age of 18 months to 5 years old. About half the children come from an English-speaking background, 20% from Spanish-speaking and 30% from a variety of other language backgrounds. Some children are multilingual.

Children aged 18 months to 3 years are taught in Spanish only. From then on, both English and Spanish are used as the medium of instruction, and it has been found that this system works well. Music is used as a central teaching device, since songs enable children to learn and remember connected language and basic vocabulary. The nursery has produced a CD called *La Mariposa Loca* which consists of songs sung in Spanish by the children and staff, with a sleeve containing the lyrics in both Spanish and English. Other activities that help children to learn in enjoyable ways include storytelling and storyreading, and the use of puppets.

Problems have been caused for the nursery by the change in UK educational policy of admitting children to primary school at 4 rather than 5 years old. This means that pre-school providers lose the grant previously available for 4 to 5-year-olds, making it harder to run a full curriculum, and children thus spend less time in bilingual education.

One aim of the nursery is to encourage children from Spanish-speaking backgrounds to feel connected with their cultural roots. These children may tend to be reserved when they enter the nursery, but they later gain confidence and become the 'language leaders'. Meanwhile, children from other language backgrounds learn Spanish quickly.

The nursery's educational philosophy is humanistic and promotes social inclusion. As well as teaching languages, the staff aim to prepare children to integrate into a multilingual and multicultural society through learning respect for others and tolerance. Establishing rapport and a warm relationship with the children is seen as an essential basis for learning to take place. Teachers look out for children's different learning styles and take account of these, whilst also introducing the child to other styles. They aim to build self-confidence.

Parents are encouraged to come into the nursery and talk to staff. They are expected to participate because their support is required for the nursery to function. Outings only take place if two parents from each class accompany the children. A parents' group does fund-raising and runs multicultural events. The nursery now also runs weekly evening classes for parents, allowing them to take a crash course in Spanish. The popular after-school Spanish clubs at primary schools in Lambeth are another support for parents and children. Those involved with the nursery hope to open a bilingual primary school to continue children's bilingual education. At present this is still a dream, driven by passion and commitment, which requires funding and support from policy makers, to give due recognition to the fact that multilingual skills are now key to future success.

Gloria Gómez can be contacted at: anglospanish98@yahoo.com

Indigenous language immersion: The challenge of meeting the needs of L1 and L2 speakers in Irish-medium pre-schools

Tina Hickey, University College Dublin

Introduction: Ireland's language policy

Over 150 regional and minority languages are spoken in the EU, by up to 50 million speakers (European Commission, 2004:9). In the Republic of Ireland, an officially bilingual state, Irish is 'the first official language' and English is also recognised as an official language. Census 2006 showed that, while about 1.66 million people (42% of the population) reported that they were 'able to speak Irish,' over 60% of these said that they 'never' speak the language or speak it less often than weekly. Even in officially designated Irish-speaking communities Irish does not appear secure, with only 57% (36,500 persons) speaking Irish daily.

Thus, Irish is both an official language and an endangered language. Efforts to maintain Irish must now also adapt to the context of the recent rise in immigration into Ireland, which has led to one of the highest levels of linguistic diversity, with 158 languages now spoken (McPake *et al*, 2007). Catering for these needs in a state already trying to maintain a minority language raises particular challenges, since the language needs of new groups can be perceived as threatening to indigenous minority languages, particularly if resources are spread too thinly.

The majority of children in the Republic now learn Irish as a single compulsory subject from school entry at age 4-5, and it is the second language for the majority. About 5% of pupils (33,000) attend the 168 primary and 43 postprimary Irish-medium schools in the Republic and Northern Ireland. In addition, there is a system of Irish-medium pre-schools (*naíonraí*) for children aged 3 to 4 years. These pre-schools have been particularly popular since they began in the 1970s, and currently serve over 3,000 children per year in 167 groups. These groups are the focus of the research discussed below.

Irish-medium preschools

Irish-medium pre-schools or *naíonraí* aim to help young children develop Irish naturally either as their mother tongue (L1) or as their second language (L2), in the context of a high quality pre-school. Evaluations (eg Hickey, 1997) showed high parental satisfaction with these pre-schools, good outcomes for Irish as L2, and an increase in the use of Irish at home.

Most effective L2 learning activities

Consideration of the most effective language learning activities in these immersion pre-schools revealed some interesting findings. The five activities that the *naíonraí* Leaders rated as the most effective for promoting Irish were: songs/rhymes, story time, home-corner, group games, and card matching. However, when Leaders were asked which activities *actually* occurred most frequently in their groups, the 'most effective' language activities were found to occur with surprisingly low frequency, while less language-centred activities received most time. This highlights the need for training for immersion educators to promote the most effective planning of language-promoting activities.

There may also need to be greater review on what the most effective activities for language learning are in the immersion setting. Observational data on the children's language use showed that role-play in the home corner appeared to be less effective in the early stages of L2 learning than the Leaders believed,

138

simply because children's limited Irish causes them to switch to English in this context. This means that activities normal to a mother tongue pre-school setting need to be adapted for an L2 immersion setting. For example, home corner play may be more effective if L2 learners are supported through some Leader input or 'scripted' support for what they wish to say, rather than being left to switch to their L1.

The activities which were found to be most successful at eliciting Irish use among the L2 learners in the *naíonraí* were the more structured ones, such as playing games with rules (eg card games or movement games), songs and rhymes, daily routines such as lunch and clean-up, and supervised activities such as art and jigsaws. This points to the need to establish a balance in immersion between these more structured activities that provide appropriate input and scaffolding for L2 learners, and free play activities that have other cognitive and social benefits.

In addition, the data pointed to a need to engage in more comprehensive and long-term work planning to ensure that children continue to make progress over the year towards a supported experience of the most language-rich activities such as role-play and storytelling. Teacher training for these immersion pre-schools has now been developed to increase awareness of the need to plan the language aspect of every activity and to promote children's Irish language development more effectively. In addition, some language support materials for parents have been developed including CDs of rhymes, songs and stories.

Concerns and challenges

One concern of recent years is that the concentration on teaching Irish as a second language to the majority of children has distracted attention from the language needs of the minority of mother tongue speakers of Irish. A small number of *naíonraí* operate in Irish-speaking communities, and here their brief is to develop these children's mother tongue skills in Irish, as well as their social and cognitive development. However, because the population of these areas is not uniformly Irish-speaking, these groups usually contain L2 learners of Irish in the same classrooms as the mother tongue speakers. These young Irish L1 speakers may not be getting the support they need, even in Irish-medium pre-schools and schools, due to a prioritisation of the needs of L2 learners. Low levels of Irish use by L1 Irish-speaking children in the *naíonra* have been found when they are doing activities without adult supervision (Hickey, 2001, 2007), and the children's Irish shows evidence of attenuation and convergence with English. Baker and Jones (1998) note that research shows that young minority language speakers need L1 enrichment to compensate for the reduced number of interlocutors and domains of use available to them and their more restricted exposure to the language.

In addition, evidence from a survey of the parents of the native speakers of Irish (Hickey, 1997) showed few literacy activities in Irish in their homes, which means that many of these Irish speaking children do not receive the enrichment of being read to in Irish regularly at home. Rather than compensating for this disadvantage, interviews with the Leaders of *naíonraí* where L1 speakers and L2 learners were mixed showed that some of them even delayed language-rich activities such as storytelling or reading to the L1 speakers until the L2 learners in the group were judged to be ready for them. Clearly a one-size-fits-all approach which prioritises the language needs of L2 learners does not promote awareness of, or provision for, the urgent needs of mother tongue minority language speakers with limited sources of input. An example is given below of the result of this approach, looking specifically at the types of input offered to the children.

Input offered

Examination of the input from adults in the *naíonra* indicates consistent attempts to simplify the language to make it accessible for L2 learners. There was a tendency to focus on helping L2 learners to acquire basic phrases, such as how to ask permission and indicate preferences, and basic body, colour and shape terms, as well as counting and the days of the week. In the example here, the Leader and her assistant are trying to get the L2 learners to use basic colour names, and in the process overlooking the language needs of the Irish L1 child (TC, target child). This example opposite gives a flavour of the language used in managing the group, the simplification for L2 learners, and the lack of differentiated provision for the L1 speaker here.

Here the language needs of the L1 Irish-speaker have not been addressed when he needs a colour term missing from his vocabulary, because the focus is on teaching basic colour terms to the L2 learners. The example also illustrates adaptation of input to simplify it for L2 learners, but such input does not offer the kind of enriched language needed by minority language L1 children.

Other data showed the tendency for mother tongue Irish speakers to switch to English when an L2 learner addressed them in English, or played in parallel to them. The children seemed to have interpreted the agenda of these pre-schools as '(try to) speak Irish to the adults, but with other kids, you can speak

Example 1[1]

Leader: *Cén dath atá ar *geansaí atá ag Liam?* What colour is Liam's jumper?
(*No marking of noun following preposition)

Leader: *Anois fan go bhfeicfidh tú anois.* Now wait till you see now
Cén dath atá ar *geansaí *Liam? What colour is Liam's jumper?
(*No marking after proposition and no genitive marking on name)

Leader: *Anois!* Now (Warning, trying to get the child's attention)

Child 1: *Bán.* White

Asst: *Anois!* Now!
(Admonishment, looking at a child who is not listening).

Child 2: *Dearg.* Red

Asst: *Bándearg!* Pink! (white-red, supplying correct term)

Child 2: *Bándearg.* Pink

Leader: *xx ar bríste atá ar *Seán?* xx on Seán's trousers?
(*No marking on name after preposition)

Child 3: *Bán.* White

Child 4: *Glas.* Green

Leader: *Glas, an dath atá ar do xx* Green, the colour of your xx.

Child 3: *Glas.* Green

Asst.: *Agus bróga *bán, bróga *bán* And *white shoes, * white shoes
(*No plural marking on adjective)
agus tá ribín uirthi, tá And she has a ribbon on her, she has.

TC: *Agus tá purple air!* And it is purple! (suddenly volunteering comment)

Asst: *Cinéal purple sea.* Sort of purple, yes

Child 2: I got xx socks. (calling her attention to his socks)

Leader: *ó tá xx deasa.*   Nice xx

1. Irish is shown in Italics, with the English translation immediately afterwards. The asterisk indicates an error or non-standard simplification of Irish morphosyntax, and 'xx' represents an inaudible or unintelligible word.

English'. Interviews with the Leaders in the pre-schools indicated some lack of awareness of the need to group the mother tongue speakers together at times, with statements such as: 'Why would I give native speakers any special attention?' and 'In my opinion the beginners are in greater need of attention.' Other research (eg Valdes, 1997) on mixed groups in immersion has highlighted the potential dangers of such attitudes for minority language speakers, with the input offered to them in mixed settings containing fewer questions, less feedback, more limited vocabulary, and more repetition than is suitable for language enrichment among native speakers of a minority language.

Applications beyond this sector

Overall, the results from Irish-medium pre-schools are positive, in offering quality pre-schooling where children make significant progress in acquiring Irish as a second language. However, minority language communities must be aware that groups or classes where mother tongue speakers are mixed with second language learners require differentiated provision. Rather than treating L1 speakers of minority languages as 'mini language teachers' for their L2 learner peers, there is a pressing need to address their own linguistic weaknesses, in order to develop a greater range of vocabulary, styles and functions in their first language, often lacking in the case of a minority language. Mixing second language learners with mother tongue minority language speakers requires us to examine the socio-linguistic factors which affect attitudes to speaking the target language, since even young children are aware of the lower status of some languages compared to others. It is essential to recognise the need to target L1 speakers' accuracy, vocabulary, self-esteem and networks, alongside helping L2 learners to acquire the language.

The Anglo European School:
How an international dimension in education enhances all-round learning
David Barrs and Jill Martin, Anglo European School, Essex

Anglo European School in Essex, Eastern England, is a secondary school with specialist Language College status. At an Ofsted inspection in 2005 the school was praised for its international approach to the curriculum, building students' self-confidence, intercultural awareness and sense of social responsibility, as well as their language skills. AES was set up in 1973 as a comprehensive school providing a European and international dimension to education. Students come from different backgrounds and currently there are up to 60 languages represented. Many staff are either trained overseas or are non-UK nationals.

AES is a values-driven school, and its internationalist ethos includes 'empathy and openness and a respect for your neighbour's right to be different'. The aim is to value one's own culture, whilst developing a critical respect for the culture of others. This approach enables students to feel confident about their own identities whilst being taught in harmony with others. Listening is emphasised as a key skill of communication, and students are encouraged to develop their ideas through discussion. Debating controversial topics is a frequent activity in the school, allowing students to see both sides of an issue, leading to an understanding of other people's points of view.

Internationalist skills are based on breadth rather than specialisation. AES has an enrichment curriculum for all students, with overseas visits and exchanges, opportunities to find out about the work of non-governmental organisations, a model UN Assembly, an ongoing commitment to a charity in India and a genuine dialogue with a variety of faith organisations which enriches the spiritual dimension of the school's work. Every student studies at least two languages as well as English, beginning with French and German, and adding Spanish, Russian, Chinese, Italian or Japanese as an enrichment language in Year 9. Latin is also available and the school runs a Polish Club. Children proficient in their mother-tongue are encouraged to enter GCSEs early in their native language. Some 13-year-olds are taught geography and history through the medium of French and German. The school tries to avoid the term 'modern foreign languages': they are neither modern nor foreign! The word 'foreign' can have negative associations, and AES students often speak other languages as their mother-tongue.

Twelve hundred students a year are involved in international exchanges: 700 from AES and 500 coming to the school from other countries. AES students go to Belgium, France, Germany, Spain and Russia, and in the sixth form they take part in World Challenge activities that can take them to places like Pakistan, Argentina, Namibia and Peru. They spend considerable lengths of time away, for example eight weeks for 14 to 15-year-olds in Germany, which frequently result in solid friendships, and help students to gain in-depth understanding of another culture.

All departments in the school are required to build a European and international outlook into the syllabus. This global curriculum culminates in the International Baccalaureate in the sixth form, including two languages as well as science, mathematics and a humanity subject, and a community/voluntary-based activity. The focus on languages and internationalism throughout a broad curriculum stimulates achievement across the board, and ethnic minority students get particularly good results in this model.

The school sees a difference between globalisation and internationalism. The former argues that we should accept global capitalism because 'this is how the world is'. The latter stems from a democratic outlook and works for change, 'because this is how we want the world to be'. The educationalist Kurt Hahn expressed the aims and ethos of Anglo European School when he said 'while we may not be able to change the world, we can produce young people who want to' (James, 2000).

Further information on the school can be obtained from David Barrs or Jill Martin (barrsd@aesessex.co.uk).

The school's website is www.aesessex.co.uk

Based on a presentation to the Multilingual Europe seminar series at Goldsmiths, University of London by Bob Reed, former headteacher, who passed away in November 2005.

7

Teacher education for diversity

This chapter shows how teacher education can benefit from the inclusion of cross-cultural perspectives, a greater variety of languages, and pedagogies adapted to multilingual learners. For example, student teachers on placement in other countries are prompted to reconsider practices and policies they might not otherwise have questioned, thus becoming reflective practitioners who improve their teaching across the board. Courses preparing teachers of minority languages need to cater for pupils with a range of proficiency levels, and the solutions arrived at to meet this challenge contribute significantly to language teaching in general. Meanwhile, raising educational achievement among pupils who are studying in a new language requires teachers to use explicit strategies that enhance cognitive academic linguistic proficiency, and also to develop the whole school as an inclusive learning community. Sharing ideas across countries can help teachers meet the needs of linguistically and culturally diverse pupils, as demonstrated by the TESSLA project, a partnership of teacher educators from Estonia, France, Germany, Sweden, Turkey and the UK.

Different countries, different pedagogies: Student teacher exchanges for primary language learning
Claudine Kirsch, Goldsmiths, University of London

I n UK primary schools, language learning will become an 'entitlement' for children aged 7 to 11 by 2010, through the National Languages Strategy (DfES, 2002b). ➡ *see also Part 3: The English National Languages Strategy p170*. To prepare for this, from 2001 the Training and Development Agency began funding five Initial Training Institutions to run a primary course with a specialism in foreign languages. By 2007/8, 41 institutions offered this course in French, Spanish, German and Italian to 945 students in the UK (NACELL, 2007). The recent Languages Review (DfES, 2007b) recommends making primary languages a compulsory subject, which calls for further developments. The government offers an annual budget of £50m to support the development of language learning (BBC, 2007), and some of this will be spent on training.

Currently, the content and allocated teaching time of primary language courses differ from institution to institution. Some offer the specialism to PGCE students (Postgraduate/ Professional Certificate in Education), others to Bachelor of Education students. Most institutions offer a thirty-hour course to undergraduates and postgraduates. What all these language specialism courses have in common is a four-week school-based placement in another country, where trainees can develop their teaching skills, language competence and intercultural understanding. In collaboration with France, Spain and Germany, the Training and Development Agency has developed a common reference framework that sets out the aims of the exchange, gives some guidance on the amount of required teaching and defines some assessment criteria (Training and Development Agency, 2007). Students are supposed to teach foreign languages, in this case English, during their exchange, as well as core and foundation subjects in the target language. Teaching content in a foreign language abroad is a daunting adventure: students need to have the necessary language and intercultural skills, to understand the educational system, to be familiar with the national curriculum and to master a range of teaching approaches, to name just a few challenges. This is difficult for an experienced teacher, let alone a student who has only had a few weeks of teaching practice and input at college before going abroad.

Goldsmiths has developed bilateral exchanges with France, Germany, and Spain for its PGCE course. The Goldsmiths team has carried out research on the period of practice abroad, through questionnaires, conversations and written work from 240 students over a period of four years. These data provide a consistent picture of the benefits and challenges of the exchange, and the most noteworthy finding is that almost every student thought the exchange was the best part of the course.

Given some of the challenges mentioned above, it is understandable that the teaching practice abroad causes high levels of anxiety, despite a good preparation at Goldsmiths. We found that prior to departure, many students thought they might be disadvantaged in comparison to their peers on the regular PGCE training route who had a whole month more to teach core and foundation subjects, to familiarise themselves with the National Curriculum and the guidance offered by the National Strategies, and to develop their subject knowledge and classroom management skills. As tutors we collaborate closely with our partner institutions and the primary schools involved to ensure the exchange helps students cover these aspects of their training. For example, we set up written agreements on the teaching load, subjects to be taught and the means and frequency of assessment.

A close rapport with students before, during and after the exchange is necessary to provide reassurance, clarify points and give assistance. We explain the educational system of the host country and outline the different teaching approaches students are likely to experience. In France, for example, all our trainees are placed with *maîtres formateurs* who are skilled in working on children's *représentations*: that is, starting with children's own mental representations of concepts and helping them move to a clearer understanding of the ideas concerned. These tutors spend two-thirds of their working time as primary school teachers and a third of their time as teacher trainers at the IUFM (*Institut Universitaire de Formation des Maîtres*). We observed year after year that the students admired the qualities and values of this approach. However, they struggled at first, preferring the structure and safety of the lessons they were used to teaching in England. They found it very hard to identify children's *représentations* and to guide them skilfully in these highly complex metacognitive activities in a second language. In order to help students deal with this challenge, we needed to work both with the students, to introduce them to social constructivist theories, and with the partner institutions, to develop clear and appropriate expectations about what students can possibly achieve.

The students' fears that they would miss out on aspects of their training because of fewer opportunities to teach in the UK proved unfounded. Instead, they all improved their teaching skills. In interviews with us, students commented that teaching in a second language was a key factor in developing a critical approach to planning. They found that they needed to be very clear about learning objectives and to plan thoroughly. They often made copious notes of instructions and key questions and thought in great detail about teaching methods. While teaching through the target language, they drew effectively on mime and gesture and used strategies such as asking children to rephrase explanations to ensure they had made themselves understood. Teaching in the target language also affected assessment and lesson evaluation. Students understood the reasons behind assessment better, and began to use their evaluations more effectively to extend children's learning and to plan future lessons.

Our view that students had improved their planning and teaching skills concurred with the data from the student questionnaires of the last four years. The vast majority indicated that they had improved their general teaching skills through adopting different teaching approaches, interacting in new ways with children and teachers (through groupwork and teamwork) and using different resources. All commented on their improved understanding of pedagogy (not just of the didactics of teaching languages), their emerging understanding of the links between curricula and pedagogy, and their knowledge of the educational system in the host country. As we hoped, they indicated having improved their subject knowledge, developed their language skills and cultural knowledge, and increased their confidence in teaching all subjects.

We agree with our partner institutions and many others involved in the exchange programme that the most essential and beneficial aspect of the exchange is the opportunity to compare systems and practices, and to look at the familiar from a different perspective. As a result, students develop a more critical approach and deepen their understanding of teaching and learning. Two examples help clarify this point.

Each year, students compared children's attitudes to learning, teaching approaches, the use of teacher assistants, classroom management, planning, material resources, funding, the organisation of schools and educational policies. Initially, many perceived the various facets of the host educational system through the filter of their own home system, which sometimes resulted in them rejecting particular features. A typical example concerns differentiation, the adaptation of teaching to suit the differing needs of pupils. Many students stated at first that teachers in the target country did not differentiate. Discussions with the class teacher and the supervising tutor helped them to clarify the concept of differentiation and explore a variety of approaches to it, and make informed decisions on grouping and collaborative learning.

Another topic that led to complex discussions was the country's approach to pupils with different cultural and linguistic backgrounds. Students understood that it was important to capitalise and build on the linguistic abilities which many pupils already possess. However, they commented that the highly centralised French national curriculum made no special provision for children who were entering school unfamiliar with the French language and culture. In the context of policies regarding cultural difference, some students who went to France vehemently rejected the teacher's approach to inclusion, describing it as assimilation. They claimed that children's cultural background was simply ignored. Some students had to overcome strong feelings about the ban on wearing religious symbols in French schools, which arose from the separation between Church and State in France that prevents religion from being brought into education.

As tutors, we discussed a range of ways to create an inclusive classroom that offers support, for example, to children whose mother tongue differs from the language used at school. We needed to provide students with opportunities to discuss the differences in the practices they had experienced and to help them understand the host culture and its educational system better. For example, students explored the emphasis on the individual in England, compared with the French republican position in which becoming a citizen is more important than being an individual. Through a comparison of the two systems and a critical analysis of the context in which each is situated, they could see more clearly why there were different approaches to inclusion. Students began to develop an awareness of the relationship between education, culture and society. They began to understand that education does not take place in a vacuum and is an important vehicle for transmitting social values.

We identified a marked shift in the students' thinking as a result of this intercultural exchange: many began to question some of their own views and to develop their understanding of key aspects of teaching and learning. They developed a more critical approach to the curriculum and approaches to teaching not only in the host country but also in their own. Having gained some distance from practices widely used in England, they also began to evaluate the English National Curriculum and the Numeracy and Literacy Strategies in what was a new and wider social, cultural and political framework. This allowed them to think more objectively and to analyse the advantages and disadvantages of both systems. As a result, they developed a much broader and less insular perspective on education.

The Head of Government Initiatives at the Training and Development Agency gave further weight to our observations when he reported that Primary Language students tend to be more reflective and critical than student teachers in general, and to think about learning and teaching differently. Thus it appears that the exchange has benefits that extend beyond the issue of teaching a target language, and promotes the development of reflective practitioners who can apply a greater level of critical thinking to all of their teaching.

The exchange has also brought benefits for tutors, by providing us with an opportunity to analyse the English, French, German and Spanish education systems. Our own teaching has taken on a broader dimension, building on these insights. We are now able to ensure that the bilateral exchange is beneficial for all students on the Initial Training courses, not just those who have taken part in it. Given the need for primary language specialists, the Training and Development Agency will continue to expand these courses. It is vital that, in answering the pressing need for competent and confident primary teachers, we aim to develop a model of excellence in training for language teaching.

I would like to thank John Wadsworth and my colleagues in the primary MFL team at Goldsmiths for their contributions to this chapter.

TESSLA: Teacher Education for the Support of Second Language Acquisition
Andrea Young, IUFM (Institut universitaire de formation des maîtres d'Alsace/Teacher Education Institute of Alsace)

ncreasing global communication and mobility is reflected in the cosmopolitan composition of many of our school populations in the new Europe. The consequent challenges facing educators in the 21st century include:

- How to create a welcoming school environment in which all children may feel at home and ready to learn
- How to develop an inclusive whole school policy which values linguistic and cultural differences
- How to support children who speak a different language at home from the language of the school
- How to encourage children whose first language is the language of the school to be tolerant, curious and to understand rather than to fear, stigmatise or ridicule difference

Providing the knowledge and the tools necessary to help educators reflect on such issues should be a vital part of teacher education and training. Regrettably this is often not the case, leaving many teachers feeling ill-equipped to teach effectively in multicultural contexts. The TESSLA project (www.tessla.org) is a partnership of educators from Estonia, France, Germany, Sweden, Turkey and the UK which tries to address these issues by proposing curricula for initial teacher education and in-service training based on holistic and multidisciplinary approaches. TESSLA's main objective is to develop materials for teachers to understand why and how they should support bilingual and multilingual children. In particular, the project addresses the questions of how to sensitise teachers to the needs of their linguistically and culturally diverse pupils, and how to equip them with strategies to support all children in their learning and create a safe classroom environment which recognises and promotes respect for diversity (Hancock *et al*, 2006).

TESSLA has achieved this through the development and piloting of a number of teacher education programmes such as the 'Home language(s)/School Languages' module. The aims of this particular pre-service course for kindergarten and primary school teachers are twofold:

- To encourage student teachers to become aware of issues associated with cultural diversity and second language acquisition (SLA), such as the complexity of bilingualism/plurilingualism, the construction of multiple identities, and the impact of linguistic policies on language maintenance and shift
- To identify strategies to support pupils' second language learning whilst at the same time promoting mutual enrichment and respect between culturally diverse pupils. Examples include introducing a language awareness approach which aims to educate all children together about the value of plurilingualism and pluriculturalism; integrating the languages and cultures of all the pupils across the whole school curriculum; and striving for greater cooperation between school and home communities

The course uses problem-based learning (PBL) in conjunction with theoretical readings and is illustrated by personal testimonies and video recordings of teachers, parents and children interacting at home and at school. A wide variety of other resources, such as music, children's literature, website materials including games and classroom ideas, have also been included to cater for all tastes and learning styles.

Evaluations of the pilot courses have revealed that the multi-modal, problem based learning and collaborative approach adopted by the course, encompassing simulation, discussion in peer groups, reading and visualising, was decisive in facilitating the adjustment of the teachers' beliefs about and attitudes towards languages and cultures, resulting in heightened intercultural sensitivity and language awareness. Further information on TESSLA is available at: http://www.tessla.org/home/

Initial teacher education for teachers of Arabic, Mandarin Chinese, Panjabi and Urdu
Jim Anderson, Goldsmiths, University of London

Goldsmiths, University of London, is one of a number of initial teacher education providers to have introduced a Secondary Postgraduate Certificate of Education (PGCE) course in minority languages (Arabic, Mandarin Chinese, Panjabi and Urdu). The decision to take this initiative was based on the belief that the language curriculum in schools needs to take account of diversity within British society, and to prepare young people for an increasingly internationalised job market and for global citizenship. It is a philosophy which sees plurilingualism or 'English plus' (CILT, 2006) as a desirable goal both for the individual and for society. Importantly, this initiative was facilitated by a more inclusive approach by government in relation to language and culture reflected in both the National Languages Strategy (DfES, 2002b) and in the revision to the Initial Teacher Training Standards introduced in the same year (Teacher Training Agency, 2002), a policy shift which is further pursued in the recent Languages Review (DfES, 2007b).

Provision for minority languages within mainstream education in the UK is limited: whilst bilingual education is supported for speakers of the Celtic languages in Wales, Scotland and Northern Ireland, and has proved successful, this opportunity has not been available for speakers of other minority languages. Some of these languages are taught as discrete subjects in mainstream secondary schools alongside French, German and Spanish; however, the main provision across primary and secondary age groups is made in the voluntary, community-based sector which operates mainly at weekends (CILT, 2005).

Minority languages and the people studying them do not form one simple homogeneous category. Whereas Urdu and Panjabi are studied predominantly by children from the minority communities, courses in Arabic and Mandarin are increasingly being provided for children from non-user backgrounds. Clearly, there are significant economic and religious factors at work here. There are also significant differences in linguistic and cultural backgrounds and in levels of exposure. For the majority of students, especially those born in Britain, English is their dominant language and their competence in the minority language may be confined largely to oral skills and to a few specific domains of use.

Course design
The Postgraduate Certificate of Education (PGCE) course in minority languages offered at Goldsmiths is modular in structure (see Table 1 below) and contains specialist subject strands as well as general professional studies strands. As a Flexible PGCE course, a substantial element of the programme

Table 7.1: Flexible PGCE course structure (Revised Sept 2007)

Modules	Description
Subject Study 1	Introduction to subject studies: supported self-study, together with compulsory attendance at college-based workshops and tutorials.
General Professional Studies	Supported self-study, together with compulsory attendance at college-based workshops and tutorials.
School Experience ☐ School Induction ☐ and Needs Analysis	10 days (normally two full weeks) pursuing a structured programme of activities. Following this an individual training plan is put in place.
☐ School Experience 1	The equivalent of 10 full weeks following a structured programme of activities and building up experience of classroom teaching.
☐ School Experience 2	12 full weeks following a programme of teaching, together with a number of directed activities.
Subject Study 2	Development of subject studies: supported self-study, together with compulsory attendance at college-based workshops and tutorials.

is delivered through supported self-study, enabling students to fit their study around other commitments. Complementing this is the compulsory pro-gramme of workshops and classes based at Goldsmiths which provides the essential elements of face-to-face teaching and collaborative learning. To-gether with the coordinating tutor, specialist tutors in the different languages make important contributions both to self-study material and to college workshops. A large part of the course is school-based and Goldsmiths works in partnership with a range of schools across different sectors. While in schools, students are supported by specialist mentors, who provide regular feedback and support. The various issues involved in finding suitable school placements are discussed below.

Students complete portfolio tasks and longer assignments at different stages during the course for assessment purposes. They are also assessed on their classroom work by school mentors and college tutors. Overall progress is re-viewed at key points during the course in relation to the government Stan-dards for Initial Teacher Training, which set out the range of competences stu-dents are expected to demonstrate in order to gain Qualified Teacher Status. The ongoing integration of theory and practice is emphasised, with the aim of developing teachers who are able to evaluate critically both the effective-ness of their classroom work and broader aspects of educational policy.

Unlike the traditional one-year PGCE course, the flexible route allows stu-dents up to two years to complete; however, a majority of students finish within eighteen months. A significant proportion of those who have taken the course so far are mature students with work or childcare commitments, for whom the one-year intensive route to the PGCE would not be a realistic option. The flexible route has also proved effective in addressing individual needs by taking account of prior experience, so that it has been possible to exempt some students from certain elements of the course.

Methodology
With regard to methodology, account needs to be taken of official frameworks for language study, in particular the National Curriculum for Modern Foreign Languages (DfEE/QCA, 1999) and the specifications for the main public examinations. However, in the case of minority community languages it is seen as essential to move beyond a narrow transactional model, shaped by the needs of the tourist, to one based on broader understandings of language and culture and taking greater account of student backgrounds. Enriching the curriculum content through links to other subject areas is seen as impor-tant; moreover, the potential of the Content and Language Integrated Learn-

ing (CLIL) approach (Coyle, 2000; Marsh, 2002) as a means of reconciling conflicting foreign language and mother tongue models of language teaching is also recognised, if little seen in practice. In line with socio-constructivist theory as well as key principles of communicative methodology, efforts are made to maximise learner engagement and control through an interactive teaching style and the opportunity to take part in collaborative work in groups. This represents a significant shift from the more formal, didactic methods most of the students have experienced in their own education.

Within the broad framework outlined above, there is scope to adapt teaching to meet the needs of different groups of learners. Where teachers are working with children from minority language backgrounds, they are able to draw on a shared knowledge of the language and culture and their personal relationship to it. This has implications for the way topics and texts are presented and worked on in the classroom. Brainstorming, for example, provides a rich context for exploring ideas and language. Teachers must also recognise that, for bilinguals, language mixing is a natural part of communication, and that insistence on the exclusive use of the target language in the classroom may be inappropriate. It is important to understand that these children are living between two or more languages and cultures, in a society where the education system is profoundly monolingual in its outlook. The minority language classroom is therefore an important space for valorisation of mixed identities. A wealth of resources from home and local community can be drawn upon to enable children to investigate aspects of culture and the interrelationship of cultures in diverse cities such as London.

Materials

A long-standing issue has been the lack of textbooks and other documentation to support teaching of minority languages and the professional development of minority language teachers. The National Curriculum and other government frameworks for language teaching are all geared towards the commonly taught European languages. In order to fill this gap a project was developed at Goldsmiths with the support of the Nuffield Foundation to create curriculum guides in Arabic, Mandarin, Panjabi, Urdu and Tamil (CILT, 2007). The guides aim to provide practical support for colleagues in planning their teaching and enabling proper recognition for children's learning. They are based on the teaching philosophy outlined above and cater for courses at primary as well as secondary level. Links are made to recent government initiatives such as the Languages Ladder delivered through the Asset Languages qualifications available in over twenty languages ➡ see *also Part 3: The Languages Ladder p175*.

Partnership with schools

In building the course we have formed partnerships with schools in the state-maintained, independent and community-based sectors. However, only a few secondary schools offer minority languages, and finding suitable placements for a growing number of students on the course has presented complications.

Firstly, the school needs to be able to allocate an appropriate number of classes for the student teacher to make up an adequate teaching load, including some larger classes of over twenty students. This is not always easy, especially where the language concerned is just being introduced onto the timetable. It is helpful if the student teacher has a second language that they can

Oracy	Literacy

• 听录音, 记下约会的细节: Listening and noting: listening to recordings of people making arrangements and noting details.
• 角色扮演 Role-play:
  – 约朋友看电影(用电话), 表达不同意见 Act out scene (on phone) where two friends disagree on what film they should go and see.
  – 扮演不同性格的人物, (如乐观 / 悲观人物) Act out scene as a people with particular character, e.g. someone very optimistic, someone very pessimistic (using finger puppets).
  – 扮演间谍 Act a spy (on the phone) arranging to meet another spy in a certain row at the cinema to pass on secret information, e.g. James Bond.
	• 排列对话顺序 Sequencing dialogue.
	• 浏览节目表 / 目录, 找出主要的讯息。 Scanning events pages in magazine or on Internet for key information.
	• 从电影介绍中找出 3 部你喜欢看的电影, 并且解释你的原因。例如: 近代作品— 《英雄》、《警察故事》经典作品— 《红楼梦》、《三国演义》 From film information, identifying three you might like to see and explain reason for your choice.

Curriculum guide for **Chinese**

Themes, topics, texts

العنصرية: سابقاً

ولاحقاً

Racism then and now

أسباب التمييز العنصري

Causes of racism

مكافحة التمييز العنصري

Preventing racism

Resources
http://www.irespect.net/
http://www.redhotcurry.com/

Above: 12. Title of Chinese curriculum guide (copyright CILT).

Top: 13. Excerpt from Level 5 of Chinese curriculum guide showing examples of suggested activities (copyright CILT)

Right: 14. Excerpt from Level 9 of Arabic curriculum guide showing examples of suggested topics (copyright CILT)

teach, such as Arabic with French. Secondly, there should be a suitably quali-fied school mentor who is able to support the student teacher in developing their skills. Since training opportunities for teachers of minority languages have been sparse, some colleagues working in schools do not have the re-quired qualifications. Fortunately the point has now been reached where some former students are able to take on a mentoring role. Thirdly, students need to be able to observe good practice on their school placements. Again, because of a lack of training opportunities, it has been difficult for colleagues to update their teaching skills so that there may be some inconsistency in the methodology promoted in college and the practice observed in schools, and this can be confusing for students.

Despite these challenges, schools have generally been keen to play their part in supporting the course. There is recognition that enabling colleagues to gain an appropriate professional qualification is essential to improving stan-dards of teaching and learning and to raising the status of minority languages in schools.

Achievements and prospects for the future

So far, 28 students have successfully completed the PGCE at Goldsmiths and recent interviews with former students who are now working in London schools highlight the significance of the course for their professional develop-ment and their confidence in delivering their subject effectively in schools (Anderson, forthcoming). However, provision for initial teacher education in minority languages across the country is patchy and this reflects, amongst other things, difficulties in finding suitable school placements.

It remains to be seen what impact the recent *Languages Review* (DfES, 2007) will have in this respect. The report envisages a significant reshaping of pro-vision for language teaching in England and Wales which, as indicated in the introduction to this chapter, will encourage a more inclusive and flexible approach. Britain's linguistic diversity is described as a 'potential national asset' and the need to promote the teaching of Eastern languages such as Mandarin and Urdu is specifically mentioned in relation to primary and secondary provision. In this context there should be great potential for courses such as the one developed at Goldsmiths to flourish.

Excellence and Enjoyment: learning and teaching for bilingual children in the primary years

Professional development materials that support the Primary National Strategy EAL programme

Jill Catlow, EAL Consultant affiliated to the National Strategies

C hildren from ethnic minority groups, including those for whom English is an additional language (EAL), are amongst the highest achieving children in UK schools. However this is not true for all children from ethnic minority backgrounds. The Department for Education and Skills (DfES) consequently launched a pilot programme in partnership with the Primary National Strategy in 2004, which was focused on raising the educational achievement of advanced learners of EAL. 'Advanced learners' are children who appear to be appropriately fluent for their age in conversational contexts, but who need support to develop the cognitive and academic language necessary for academic success.

The pilot programme aimed to promote a wider understanding of EAL pedagogy and bilingualism across local authorities and schools; to support teachers to apply that knowledge in their daily practice; and to develop learning and teaching which would close the gap in attainment between underachieving bilingual learners and children whose first language is English. A team which included the headteacher, the literacy and mathematics coordinators and the EAL coordinator was established to lead this whole-school programme. Underachieving individuals and groups and key areas of the curriculum were identified, and pupil progress was tracked and regularly reviewed.

Recognising that all learners are affected by their social and cultural context, particular consideration was given to the development of the school as an inclusive learning community where all children feel safe, valued and secure, with a sense of belonging. A school teaches in three ways: by what it teaches, how it teaches and the kind of place it is.

The professional development materials (booklets, fliers, a CD Rom and a DVD) outline EAL pedagogy and the role of first language in learning. They provide guidance and a wealth of practical strategies within a clear structured framework: on integrated planning for language and curriculum content, assessment for learning, culture and identity, ensuring an inclusive ethos, and developing partnerships with parents, carers, families and communities.

The programme emphasises the advantages offered by bilingualism, and the significant and continuing role of the bilingual child's first language in their identity, learning and development of English.

Other key messages are:

- children learning an additional language can become conversationally fluent in 2-3 years, but take longer to develop the cognitive and academic language they need to achieve in Key Stage 2 and above

- EAL learners are potentially as able as other children, and need contextual and linguistic support to access tasks at an appropriate level of cognitive challenge

- to avoid EAL learners staying within a narrow range of familiar vocabulary, they need planned intervention to introduce new language items and planned opportunities to use new language

- EAL learners need specific support to ensure they fully comprehend what they are reading in order for new linguistic forms to become part of their repertoire

Following a positive evaluation by the NFER, the programme was rolled out nationally. The materials, useful for anyone working with bilingual learners in the primary years can be ordered from DCSF Publications: Ref: 0013-2006PCK-EN, or are available online at:

www.standards.dfes.gov.uk/primary/publications/inclusion/bi_children

8
Systems and Policies

European Union policies now encourage plurilingualism in a wide range of languages for all EU citizens. The contributions in this chapter show that steps have been taken towards this aim, but there is still some way to go. Positive moves include the change from a functional view of language to a more humanistic view that sees the value of multilingualism for personal development and social inclusion. This is particularly significant in societies such as the UK where a world language is spoken, and where until now, monolingualism for most citizens appeared to be the accepted norm. The role of assessment is crucial in validating progress in language learning, and more flexible tools are being developed that assess different language skills and offer comparable accreditation across a broad range of languages, including regional and minority languages. However, a review of language teaching in primary and secondary education in six states shows that minority languages are still competing for resources against European languages which have higher status. Finally, the influential VALEUR project shows the range, and in many cases the paucity, of provision of support for minority languages across the EU.

National strategies on language
in the European context
Claudine Kirsch, Goldsmiths, University of London

L anguage learning programmes do not exist in a vacuum, but are influenced by geographical, societal, economic and political factors. In Europe, the integration of new member states into the European Union and the wide range of languages spoken require a programme that addresses plurilingualism and linguistic diversity. This programme is expected to further mutual understanding, mobility, democratic citizenship, and social cohesion (Beacco and Byram, 2003). Since January 2007, the European Union has recognised 21 official languages, but in addition, it is estimated that 40 million EU citizens also speak one or more of the 60 languages covered by the European Charter for Regional or Minority Languages (Council of Europe, 1992). The European Union is multilingual in a double sense: first, because a range of language varieties are spoken within particular geographical areas, and second, because many of its residents are plurilingual. To promote plurilingualism and language diversity, the European Commission launched an Action Plan in 2003 (European Commission, 2003). Some of the successful initiatives implemented in primary and secondary schools are described here, as well as some of the discrepancies that remain between EU member states in their language teaching, particularly with regard to the teaching of regional or minority languages.

Plurilingual Europeans

A considerable momentum was created in 2000 when the Lisbon European Council set the target for Europe to become the most competitive and dynamic knowledge-based economy in the world. In order to accomplish this, the 2002 Barcelona European Council promoted multilingualism by recommending that all citizens become proficient in two languages other than their mother tongue (European Commission, 2003:4). Promoting language diversity meant offering opportunities to learn European and non-European languages, including regional, minority and migrant languages, known as community languages in England. The action plan had several strands:

■ Extending opportunities for life-long language learning to all citizens: eg all EU member states should offer the opportunity of beginning the study of a range of languages at primary school, continuing throughout life

162

- Improving language teaching: eg teachers in all EU member states should use a holistic approach to language teaching that helps learners make connections between their mother tongue and other languages
- Building a language-friendly environment: eg EU member states should use the media and information and communication technologies to promote language and cultural awareness
- Developing a framework for progress: eg EU member states should facilitate effective sharing of information between policy makers and practitioners

The suggested initiatives included research studies, conferences, seminars, the development of training material, e-learning, the strategic use of the education and training programmes (eg Socrates) and Town-Twinning. The Common European Framework of Reference and the European Language Portfolio are described here. They are both initiatives that encourage learners to assess their progress in any language to whatever level of competence they have acquired.

The Common European Framework of Reference (CEFR)

The Common European Framework (Council of Europe, 2001), which is available in over 30 languages, supports the organisation of language courses, facilitates the comparison of educational certificates, and eases professional mobility. The document describes the competences required for a range of social environments, sets out the aims and objectives of language teaching, and examines implications for the curriculum.

There are six *Common Reference Levels* describing a learner's competences in listening, speaking, interaction, reading and writing at successive stages. They fall into three broader divisions:

Basic learner		Independent learner		Proficient learner	
A1	A2	B1	B2	C1	C2
Breakthrough	Waystage	Threshold	Vantage	Effective operational proficiency	Mastery

---

Examples of the competences required at different levels

Listening A1

'I can understand familiar words and very basic phrases concerning myself, my family and immediate concrete surroundings when people speak slowly and clearly.'

Spoken Interaction B1

'I can deal with most situations likely to arise whilst travelling in an area where the language is spoken. I can enter unprepared into conversation on topics that are familiar, of personal interest or pertinent to everyday life (eg family, hobbies, work, travel and current events).'

Writing C1

'I can express myself in clear, well-structured text, expressing points of view at some length. I can write about complex subjects in a letter, an essay or a report, underlining what I consider to be the salient issues. I can select a style appropriate to the reader in mind.'

Several countries now use the CEFR to define learners' levels of attainment (European Commission, 2007). Thirteen member states have already changed or are in the process of changing their language curriculum and school-leaving examinations in second or foreign languages, which will facilitate comparison of achievements across Europe. A first survey of students' competences in two languages at the end of compulsory schooling will be carried out in 2010.

Although informative, the level descriptors are still too vague for teachers or textbook authors. In the last years, educationalists have therefore begun to draw up language-specific descriptions based on these six levels. These *Reference Level Descriptions* (RLD) identify the aspects of language a learner needs to master, such as grammar and vocabulary, to develop the competences described above. So far, the complete RLD have been published for Spanish and German and several levels for French and Italian.

European Language Portfolio

The European Language Portfolio (ELP) is linked to the Common European Framework (Council of Europe, 2001). It gives a holistic picture of learners' experiences, understanding and skills, and takes account of all languages learned in a range of contexts. Learners can assess their own achievements in mother tongue or community languages as well as foreign languages.

The ELP comprises three sections: the Language Passport, the biography and the dossier. The Language Passport summarises learners' self-assessed achievements against the CEFR Reference Levels. Adults can complete an electronic version called Europass. The biography encourages learners to reflect on their experience of learning and using languages and helps them to plan and assess their progress. The dossier encourages them to collect documents, pictures or recordings in order to illustrate their experiences and competences.

In 2004, 31 states were engaged in piloting and implementing the ELP (CILT/ NACELL, 2006). The English Junior version is based on the Key Stage 2 framework (DfES, 2005) and pupils can use the 'can-do' statements of the Languages Ladder ➡ *see also Part 3: The Languages Ladder p175*.

Diversity of language policies and language provision within Europe

The Eurobarometer survey (European Commission, 2006b) has confirmed that Europeans mainly learn languages in schools, indicating that good language education policies are therefore essential. Although many European countries have adapted language teaching to the Council of Europe's language policies, huge differences remain, both within and between member states (European Commission, 2007). Edelenbos *et al* (2006) have analysed the aims, models and outcomes of language learning programmes across Europe and distinguished four situations:

- ■ language awareness models with the aim of developing metalinguistic awareness and intercultural sensitivity and with modest aims regarding proficiency

- ■ language competence models that aim to develop language proficiency

- ■ more flexible programmes aiming at the development of language proficiency and encouraging links with other subjects

- ■ bilingual or plurilingual education where two or more languages, such as children's mother tongue and a second language, are used as medium of instruction ➡ *see also Part 3: Arabic/Hebrew bilingual schools p130, Anglo-Spanish Nursery School p136, Indigenous language immersion p137*.

The bilingual/plurilingual model is most effective since it gives pupils more exposure to the target language and meaningful opportunities to use their newly acquired language skills (Johnstone, 2001). Examples include schools offering bilingual education through Welsh in Wales, Gaelic in Scotland and Irish in Northern Ireland and the Republic of Ireland. In Welsh-medium schools pupils are taught exclusively in Welsh up to the age of 7, when English is introduced as a subject and may be used as a language of instruction for some aspects of the curriculum. In France, some teachers use regional languages such as Basque, Breton, Catalan, Occitan/Langue d'Oc and Corsican alongside French as their medium of instruction. In Finland, bilingual education is offered in Swedish, and in Norway and Sweden some schools in border areas offer bilingual provision. Twinned towns have developed a common curriculum and promote the teaching of neighbouring languages and the exchange of teachers.

Secondary schools in some countries (eg Estonia, France, Germany, Lithuania, Slovenia and Spain) are providing Content and Language Integrated Learning (CLIL), where a second or foreign language is used as a medium of instruction for one or two school subjects. These classes are sometimes called *European sections* (European Commission, 2007:10). CLIL offers greater input and opportunities for pupils to learn and use the language, and nurtures confidence. This provision is growing in many European primary and secondary schools, but as yet only a minority of students are involved.

The Commission's 2007 Report shows further differences across Europe with respect to the position of languages in the curriculum, the organisation of language teaching including time allocation, student participation rates and starting age, teacher education and the range of languages taught. Some countries offer a wide range of languages, including regional or minority languages or languages used in neighbouring countries such as Croatian in Slovenia, Finnish in Norway and Czech in Germany and Austria. Languages of immigrant populations also feature in some curricula, as in the case of Urdu in Scotland, Turkish in Germany and the Netherlands, and Arabic in Belgium, France and the Netherlands. In Finland, instruction is offered in 52 languages, the most widely taught being Somali and Albanian.

Although a range of languages may be taught in principle in many EU countries, they are not always offered by schools. Possible reasons include lack of staff, of financial resources or of interest. In the following two sections the focus is on the teaching of foreign languages in secondary and primary schools. European policies in support of community language learning are examined in the next part of this chapter. Readers interested in the teaching of foreign languages in higher education or adult learning should consult the Commission's 2007 report.

Foreign language teaching in secondary schools

The teaching of foreign languages is compulsory in most countries apart from the United Kingdom and Italy, though a foreign language may be required for entry to certain third-level courses. Although the aim is for EU secondary students to learn two foreign languages, fewer than half currently do so. English is the most frequently learned language, followed by French, German, Spanish and Russian. On average, students have 90 hours of foreign language teaching a year, which corresponds to 10-15% of the overall teaching time. However, there are wide variations across countries. Most teachers are specialists and have a university degree in the language they teach.

In England, the recommendation to take language off the compulsory curriculum for 14 to 16-year-olds has led to a rapid decline in students studying for national examinations at this point (DFES, 2002a). From 2004 to 2006, the number of examination entries for French and German dropped each year by 14% (Smithers and Whitford, 2006). Interest in Spanish remained more stable. Surveys showed that less than 50% of students were studying a language at this stage in the majority of state secondary schools (BBC News, 2006).

Foreign language teaching in primary schools

Over recent years, most member states have reformed their primary, and in some cases even their pre-school education, to offer the teaching of foreign languages to pupils at an early age. Approximately 50% of primary pupils in the EU member states were learning at least one foreign language by 2003/4 (Eurydice, 2005). In Luxembourg, Estonia, Sweden, Ireland, Finland, and Iceland, some children even learn two languages. English is taught most widely, followed by German or French.

The starting age for language teaching has tended to fall. Provision starts in grade 1 (children aged 5-6) in some countries (eg Malta, Norway, Luxembourg) and even before primary school in France and in some autonomous communities in Spain. However, the majority of pupils are introduced to foreign languages at the ages of 8-9 or 10-11. Where language teaching is compulsory, lessons generally last from thirty to fifty minutes. This is less than 10% of the overall teaching time. The majority of language teachers are primary teachers, thus generalists.

England is the last EU country to make foreign language learning compulsory at primary school. By 2010, every child will have the opportunity to learn an additional language from ages 7-11 (DFES, 2007b). The Key Stage 2 Framework for Languages (DfES, 2005) is an inclusive document that encourages teachers to introduce children to a range of languages, including community languages.

Conclusion

Analysis of differences in language learning provision, particularly for regional and minority languages, at primary and secondary schools shows considerable variation across EU member states. The 2007 review of the European action plan (European Commission, 2007) revealed a general consensus about the need for the development of language learning competence throughout life, the teaching of two languages in initial education, effective teaching, transparent assessment procedures and certificates. However, an increase in the range of languages offered remains an area for development. In principle, all member states have policies guaranteeing the provision of two foreign languages, some even for primary education. In principle, many member states also provide some instruction in recognised minority languages. Promising practices have been reported in the context of bilingual education or CLIL. However, in reality, most schools continue to offer English and a couple of languages from other European countries. Schools in countries where regional and minority languages are on the curriculum and that are therefore in the position to teach these languages, often do not do so. The European Commission continues to target the development of a range of languages, and the new Culture Programme for 2007-2013, which promotes cultural and linguistic diversity, will hopefully support this initiative.

European policies in support of
community language learning

*Joanna McPake, Scottish CILT (Centre for Information
on Language Teaching and Research)*

I n English, the term 'community languages' is used to refer to all languages other than the dominant, national or official language of a given society (McPake *et al*, 2007). However, this term is not widely understood elsewhere in Europe, nor do there appear to be equivalent terms in other European languages. Thus, although recent languages education policies from both the European Union and the Council of Europe have relevance for community languages, we have to infer this from statements about what are variously referred to as 'regional or minority', 'migrant' or 'non-territorial' languages, among other terms.

Historically, policy in support of community language learning was addressed in various contexts, but entirely separately from policy in support for modern foreign language learning, the latter being seen as part of wider educational policy, while community language learning was considered under a variety of policy headings such as minority rights, labour mobility or social inclusion. Only in the present decade has there been a shift to a more comprehensive approach, following the emergence of the concept of plurilingualism, and recognition that competence in languages in addition to the major national languages of Europe is valuable and should be supported and promoted.

Thus, the European Union's (2003) *Promoting Language Learning and Linguistic Diversity: An Action Plan 2004-2006* takes as its starting point the need for enhanced communication skills in an enlarged European Union of 450 million people from diverse linguistic and cultural backgrounds. The range of languages to be learned needs to include not only the 'smaller' national languages of member states, but also other kinds of languages, including regional, minority and migrant languages, and the languages of major trading partners around the world.

The Council of Europe's *Draft Guide to the Development of Language Policy Documents in Europe* (Beacco and Byram, 2003) similarly redefines, more comprehensively, the range of languages Europeans should learn. No longer should emphasis be placed exclusively on the national language of the state in which one was living, plus one or pre-ferably two national languages of other European countries, but instead on a much wider range of languages, 'encompassing the 'mother' tongue, the national language(s), regional and minority languages, European and non-European languages, etc' (p39).

European nations are now incorporating provision for community lan-guages into school curricula in different ways. For example, in Hungary which has a long tradition of bilingual education for pupils from in-digenous minority groups, similar provision has recently been made for children of Chinese descent. In the Czech Republic, widely-spoken community languages such as Vietnamese and Ukrainian are taught as school subjects during school hours. In Finland, municipalities are re-quired to offer after-school provision for community languages when more than four speakers of the same language request this. In the Netherlands, the European Languages Portfolio has been developed to enable children who speak community languages to record their skills and have these recognised by their schools.

The English National Languages Strategy in a European context: A personal view
Lid King, Director, National Languages Strategy, DCSF (Department for Children, Schools and Families)

t is a truism to say that multilingualism, and, more broadly multicultura-lism, are central features of our 21st century global societies, specifically in Europe. From the impact of international corporations such as that styling itself the 'world's local bank', through the common global experience pro-vided by sport and the arts, to major everyday changes in diet, leisure and employment opportunities, multiculturalism is an inescapable feature of our lives. Almost any national or international policy document will probably begin from this particular presupposition, even if views diverge considerably about the nature of the supposed shared meanings of our brave new world.

For while globalisation provides unprecedented opportunities, it also offers new risks and major challenges, not least in education. As early as 1964, Sterne was referring to the challenges posed by the introduction of languages into what was still an essentially nineteenth century 'monocultural, mono-linguistic and ethnocentric' education system. The 'internationalisation' of education, making it fit for purpose in the global era, remains a major challenge, and although we have certainly made some progress since Sterne's time, new challenges have emerged.

In this period of ever greater mobility, increasingly open markets and mass travel, the languages agenda bears a key relationship to such central issues as cultural and individual identity, the improvement of educational provision and standards, and social inclusion. Beyond this, languages are also a key competence enabling economic opportunities for individuals, fostering trade, maintaining social cohesion and having an impact on matters of war and peace. The challenge is the extent to which this complex relationship is understood, by practitioners and academics on the one hand, and by policy makers on the other.

Language policy in Europe

In Europe, language policy has traditionally focused on the economy and on mobility and has been very much connected with the construction of the Single European Market. Perhaps the most significant EU languages policy document of the last two decades was the *White Paper on the Learning Society* (European Commission, 1996). It set out a sweeping analysis of the impact of the information society, internationalisation and scientific and technical development, and proposed a future strategy based on broad-based knowledge and employability. Its fourth general objective was 'proficiency in three Community languages', which it described as 'a precondition if citizens of the European Union are to benefit from the occupational and personal opportunities open to them in the border-free single market' (p67).

This objective, later refined to that of 'mother tongue plus two' has been the basis for much Community policy since 1996, including the Year of Languages in 2001, and the major language programmes (Lingua, Socrates, Leonardo, Erasmus and Grundtvik). It was taken further by the Lisbon Presidency conclusions (March 2000) which agreed the need to establish a European framework to develop new basic skills including foreign languages, and by the 2002 meeting of Heads of State in Barcelona which made a political commitment to improve the mastery of basic skills, in particular by teaching two foreign languages to all from a very early age. Since then this has been the driving slogan of European Union language policy, culminating in the Action Plan *Promoting Language Learning and Linguistic Diversity* (European Commission, 2003) and the *New Framework Strategy for Multilingualism* (European Commission, 2005).

As well as continuity, there has been some noticeable change since 1996, much of it encapsulated in the *New Framework Strategy for Multilingualism.* There is a recognition that 'languages of the EU' go beyond 'European languages', and this is reflected in the new *Lifelong Learning Programme* (European Commission, 2006a) which supports key world and immigrant languages as well as the official European ones.

In itself, this change could be seen as simply an extension of the original functional, economic orientation of Europe's language policy. Yet, although this focus has been maintained, as exemplified in the recent work of the so-called 'High Level Committee', current EU perspectives take a much broader approach and seek to promote deeper significance for languages as an agent of change. In addition to competitiveness and mobility, the *Framework Strategy* presents a very strong case for language as a source of solidarity, mutual understanding and diversity, as set out in the *Charter of Fundamental Rights of the European Union* (EU, 2000). It also addresses the issue of literacy and cognitive gain:

> The ability to understand and communicate in more than one language is a desirable life-skill for all European citizens. It encourages us to become more open to other people's cultures and outlooks, improves cognitive skills and strengthens learners' mother tongue skills; it enables people to take advantage of the freedom to work or study in another Member State. (EU, 2000:II.I.I)

In some senses this developed EU perspective is much closer to the rather more humanistic traditions of the Council of Europe, an organisation which has made a major contribution to language policy and language learning, teaching and assessment for over half a century. Of particular recent importance has been the Council's (2001) *Common European Framework of Reference* which is based on an important rationale for language learning in the 21st century. Quoting the Council of Ministers it states

> ..that the rich heritage of diverse languages and cultures in Europe is a valuable common resource to be protected and developed and that a major educational effort is needed to convert that diversity from a barrier to communication into a source of mutual enrichment and understanding. (Council of Europe, 2001:1)

This illustrates a broader view of languages, as something more than, although inclusive of, a basic skill for communication, mobility and economic progress. This is an issue to which I will return after examining some aspects of UK, and specifically English language policy.

Debates and policy in the UK

The UK has always been regarded as something of a special case as far as languages are concerned. Fundamentally this has been to do with the increasingly obvious role of English as a world language, or *lingua franca*. This particular role of English has always made it less likely that public perception or national policy would ascribe to foreign language competence the overriding functional importance that it has had in many other countries. It is therefore an irony that what is increasingly regarded as the international success of English (Crystal, 1997; Graddol, 2006) may actually have led to a convergence of views about the importance of languages as something more than a useful skill.

Until recently, the broadly accepted view of languages in the UK was, in line with the functional European view, that languages are an important skill, useful for communication, including trade, and for cultural enrichment, but not essential in the way that English literacy is essential. This view has had an obvious impact on the place of languages in the school curriculum. Since the late 1990s, however, there has been a wide-ranging debate, given significant impetus by the Nuffield Languages Inquiry (2000), which has questioned some of our national pre-suppositions, and edged towards a more comprehensive rationale for a language policy.

In 2001 – the European Year of languages- there were major discussion around policy statements in England, Scotland and Wales as well as both official and unofficial responses to Nuffield. The *Agenda for Languages* document (King and Johnstone, 2001), produced to coincide with the Year, summed up a more coherent vision of languages, describing language competence as a functional skill of importance for the economy, but also as something more significant for 21st century society. It identified a risk that contemporary interest in languages could be limited to short-term economic needs, rather than being based on a long-term vision. This Agenda sees languages as a resource to be valued, and seeks to promote language learning throughout all stages of education and training. It argues against a deeply rooted assumption that English monolingualism is enough to meet the communicative aspirations of modern society. Instead it argues that 'multilingualism is better', for individuals, in terms of their sense of self and their life opportunities, for countries and states, for business and for communities. According to the Agenda, an understanding of languages, linked to openness to other cultures, helps peace and growth, trade and social inclusion. Such sentiments are also to be found reflected in the main public policy statements of the time – the Scottish *Citizens of a Multilingual World* (Ministerial Action

173

Group on Languages, 2000), the Welsh *Languages Count* (Welsh Assembly Government, 2002) and the English *National Strategy*, with its unequivocal statement that languages are 'an essential part of being a citizen' (DfES, 2002b:5).

Vision and the realities of policy

Faced with ever more complex international challenges, ideologically at least, the European and UK visions of languages have begun to converge. Such clarity of vision is important and such convergence is positive. There are, nevertheless, risks that arise if this shared vision becomes blurred. For throughout all the debates on language policy one can sense a tension between the essentially functional view of language, as a route to economic opportunities of various kinds, and a more educational or socio-cultural emphasis, which puts a premium on human relationships and understanding – in 21st century speak, on 'citizenship'.

Clearly, these ideas are not incompatible but neither are they the same. Indeed, this distinction raises a major concern about the vision of 'languages for all', for if language capability is to be exclusively concerned with the functional domain, it is likely that its impact will be more limited than if it is also about communication for mutual understanding and intercultural comprehension. The first remains at the level of an important skill, while the second says something about being human. Rather more worrying in an English speaking society, the functional rationale may actually restrict access to languages, on the grounds that, in practice, not everyone needs such hard-won skills (see Williams, 2000). We may be justifying, not a democratisation through languages, but the emergence of a new linguistic elite who have had exclusive access to multilingual education and opportunities.

How can we move forward? I think that we must combine our vision with a certain pragmatism. If linguists and champions of multilingualism argue for languages in isolation, they risk being cut off from what policy makers regard as mainstream. It is a question not of confusing the vision but of showing how it links to the key high level concerns of our 21st century societies. In England, for example, language policy must relate to some of our principal educational and social drivers, such as standards (of attainment), personalisation (of learning) and social cohesion. Otherwise, we remain in the arena of academic debate which has no impact on policy or people's daily lives.

Potential solutions

Fortunately this is not such an outrageous idea. Many aspects of our current languages strategy support such major educational objectives. Increasingly, the link between foreign language learning, mother tongue proficiency and cognitive development is becoming known (as witness the EU *Framework for Multilingualism*). Our recently developed *Key Stage 2 Framework for Languages* explicitly supports such major policy drivers as literacy, personalisation and international understanding. The *Languages Ladder* (DfES, 2005) underpins both standards and inclusion, an approach which promotes equal status for all languages.

More recently, the *Languages Review* (Dearing and King, 2006) has added weight to this 'pragmatic vision' of languages as a key component in a civilised society, with its clear view and image of languages as an enfranchisement, and its support for both opportunity and inclusivity and the importance of all languages. Let me conclude therefore by quoting from the *Review*:

> For today's young people languages matter; they are an investment that can enrich their lives socially, culturally and economically. They are a personal enfranchisement; an entitlement for all and one that recognises the distinctive learning needs of every child ... Language is the emergent property of the human will to communicate. (Dearing and King, 2006:21)

The Languages Ladder and Asset Languages:
A new assessment framework for languages in England
Karen Ashton, Cambridge Assessment

One of the overarching objectives of England's National Languages Strategy (DfES, 2002b) was the introduction of a voluntary recognition scheme. The Department for Education and Skills' (DfES) *Languages Ladder* consists of four series of 'can do' statements, one each for listening, speaking, reading and writing, against which students and teachers can informally assess progress at seventeen grades. Cambridge Assessment (formerly UCLES) was awarded the tender to develop assessments against the Languages Ladder in October 2003 by the DfES. These assessments are offered under the brand name of *Asset Languages*, and are designed to complement existing qualification frameworks in the UK and the Common European Framework of Reference (Council of Europe, 2001).

The scheme is available for all age groups within primary, secondary and post-16 educational sectors in England. There are separate assessments in listening, speaking, reading and writing across a wide range of languages including, but not limited to, Arabic, Bengali, Cantonese, Cornish, French, German, Gujarati, Hindi, Irish, Italian, Japanese, Mandarin Chinese, Modern Greek, Panjabi, Polish, Portuguese, Russian, Somali, Spanish, Swedish, Tamil, Turkish, Urdu, Welsh and Yoruba. For each of these languages, learners can choose to take a formally recognised Asset Languages qualification, *External Assessment,* or an informal assessment, *Teacher Assessment* which leads to a Grade Award by the classroom teacher, or both forms of assessment. *Teacher Assessments* are available at grade level while *External Assessments* are offered at six stages of the Languages Ladder. These stages are Breakthrough, Preliminary, Intermediate, Advanced, Proficiency and Mastery. Assessments will be available at all six stages for some languages only. Assessments represent progression in terms of functional language proficiency, as exemplified in the next section, and the six stages of *External Assessments* are broadly aligned to the six well-defined levels of the Common European Framework of Reference ➡ *see Part 3: National strategies on language in the European context p162*. In addition to accrediting language ability and rewarding learners' positive achievement, these small steps of progression represent a motivational learning ladder, providing teachers with the opportunity to use assessments formatively.

Recognition and valuing achievement in all languages

As assessments are designed to assess functional language proficiency, ie what learners *can do* in a language, they are also designed to be broadly comparable, in terms of this functional level across languages at each stage. Achieving Breakthrough, the first stage, should have the same transparent meaning across languages. For example, a learner who has achieved Breakthrough in Urdu writing should be able, broadly, to do the same things as a learner who has achieved Breakthrough in Spanish writing. This functional comparability has the advantage of providing learners, teachers and other users with a common discourse to discuss learner achievement in line with the Common European Framework of Reference levels. As well as increased transparency, having functional comparability in the assessment framework places equal academic value on learner achievement across all languages.

Additional value also comes from the increased provision of assessments, which allows more learners to have their skills accredited and valued. Prior to this scheme there were no assessment opportunities for learners of Somali, Yoruba, Tamil, Swedish and Hindi. Teachers using Asset Languages assessments have been positive about this change. One teacher commented 'we feel it's important to recognise the language. We already offer Arabic, Bengali and Turkish and wanted to give our Somali-speaking students access to a qualification as well'. The increased flexibility created by a larger number of finer-grained assessment opportunities is also viewed as positive, eg. 'we have found it motivating for pre-GCSE Urdu'.

The scheme also enables learners to be accredited at different stages for different skills, allowing them to have a jagged profile across skills or to be assessed in one or two skills only. As one teacher said, the scheme has enabled her students to be accredited at a higher stage for Panjabi listening and speaking than for writing and reading, rather than delaying accreditation until learners were equally proficient in all four skills. Given the association between under-assessment and the lowering of expectations and motivation for community language learners (see for example Datta, 2000), increased assessment opportunities play an important role in allowing language achievement in all languages to be recognised and valued both by the learners themselves and by the wider community.

Asset Languages research

Given the complexity of the assessment framework, an extensive research agenda has been set up. One area of current research is comparability across languages. Whilst the benefits of functional comparability have been outlined, ensuring comparability across assessments is not an easy task. Challenges exist, for example, in the nature of comparison when languages have different writing systems or scripts and hence different learning loads for native English speakers. For certain languages maintaining functional comparability may be undesirable if the increased time it takes for the learner to reach a particular level has a detrimental effect on motivation.

As part of this research on comparability, we are working closely with language learners and teachers. Self-assessment surveys have been used as a research tool to look at what learners *can do* in a language. Early results from one ongoing research project have shown that community language learners rated their ability as lower than that of learners of modern foreign languages working at the same level of proficiency. While the nature of the finer-grained assessments is already appreciated by teachers, there is still work to do to ensure that community language learners recognise and value their achievement in a way that is comparable to that of modern foreign language learners. As McPake (2006:63) has commented, we can hope that in future 'unhelpful distinctions between 'modern', 'foreign', 'lesser-used' languages, 'languages other than English' etc will have disappeared, and all languages will be valued for the unique contribution each can make'.

Cross-national perspectives on community language teaching in six European cities
Kutlay Yagmur, Tilburg University

Comparative study of community language teaching

I n the European public discourse on migrant groups, two major characteristics emerge: migrant groups have tended to be referred to as *foreigners* (*étrangers, Ausländer*) and as being in need of integration (Extra and Verhoeven, 1998). It has been common practice to refer to migrant groups in terms of *non-national* residents and to their languages in terms of *non-territorial, non-regional, non-indigenous,* or *non-European* languages. The call for integration is in sharp contrast with the language of exclusion. This conceptual exclusion rather than inclusion in the European public discourse derives from a restrictive interpretation of the notions of citizenship and nationality. While recent EU policy statements now include the languages of migrant groups, known as immigrant minority languages, as well as including regional minority languages, what actually takes place on the ground in different cities around Europe can diverge from the aspiration of policy initiatives. Here, the major outcomes of a comparative study on immigrant minority language teaching in Göteborg, Hamburg, The Hague, Brussels, Lyon and Madrid (Extra and Yagmur, 2002, 2004) are discussed. These findings derive from the Multilingual Cities Project, the aims of which were to gather, analyse, and compare multiple data on the status of immigrant minority languages.

In all the cities involved in this study, there had been an increase in the number of migrant pupils in primary and secondary education speaking a language at home other than, or in addition to, the dominant school language (ie a community language). Schools had responded to this home-school language mismatch by paying more attention to the learning and teaching of the mainstream language, such as English, French or Dutch, as a second language. A great deal of energy and money was being spent on developing curricula, teaching materials, and teacher training for such mainstream second-language education. Community language teaching stood in stark contrast to this, as it was much more susceptible to an ideological debate about its legitimacy. While there was consensus about the necessity of investing in second-language education for migrant pupils, there was little support for community language teaching.

Immigrant languages were commonly considered sources of problems and deficiencies, and rarely seen as a source of knowledge and enrichment. Policy makers, local educational authorities and teachers of regular subjects were often negative about community language teaching. On the other hand, parents of immigrant pupils, community language teaching teachers and migrant organisations often made a case for including immigrant languages in the school curriculum. These differences in top-down and bottom-up attitudes were found in all the cities and countries investigated.

Here, a cross-national overview of the study's findings on community language teaching in primary and secondary education is presented under the following headings: the target groups involved, arguments, objectives, evaluation, minimal enrolment, curricular status, funding, teaching materials, and teacher qualifications.

Target groups

The target groups for community language teaching in primary schools were commonly migrant children, defined as such in a narrow or broad sense. The most restrictive set of languages was taught in Spain, i.e., Arabic and Portuguese only, for Moroccan children and Portuguese-speaking children, respectively. A wide range of languages was taught in Sweden and Germany, while Belgium and France took an intermediate position. Sweden and France required the target groups to be actively using the languages at home and to have a basic proficiency in these languages. The Netherlands abolished community language teaching in primary schools in 2004, yet schools were offering Arabic, Russian, Spanish, and Turkish as modern foreign languages open to all students from all ethnic backgrounds.

Arguments

The arguments for community language teaching were formulated in terms of a struggle against deficit or in terms of multicultural policy. Whereas the former type of argument predominated in primary education, the latter type predominated in secondary education. Deficit arguments were phrased in terms of bridging the home/school gap, preventing educational failure, or overcoming marginalisation. Multicultural arguments were phrased in terms of promoting cultural identity and self-esteem, promoting cultural pluralism, promoting multilingualism in a multicultural and globalising society, and avoiding ethnic prejudice. Whereas in the Netherlands and Belgium deficit arguments dominated, multicultural arguments tended to play a greater role in the other countries.

Objectives

The objectives of community language teaching in primary schools were rarely specified in terms of language skills to be acquired. Active bilingualism was a common objective in Sweden, whereas in Germany and Spain, reference was made to the development of oral and written language skills, language awareness, and intercultural skills. In contrast, the objectives of community language teaching in secondary schools were commonly specified in terms of oral and written skills to be reached at intermediate stages and/or at the end of secondary schooling.

Evaluation

The evaluation of achievement in community language teaching took place informally and/or formally. Informal evaluation took place by means of subjective oral and/or written teachers' impressions or comments, meant for parents at regular intervals, eg once per semester or year. Formal evaluation took place using more or less objective language proficiency measurement and language proficiency report figures, eg once per semester or year. Informal evaluation tended to occur in lower grades of primary schooling, and formal evaluation in higher grades (eg in Sweden). In most countries, however, no school grades were given throughout the primary school curriculum. If school grades were given (eg in France), such marks commonly did not have the same status as grades for other subjects. The evaluation of achievement through community language teaching in secondary schools took place formally through assessment instruments and examinations. Here, course grades had a regular or peripheral status. The former held in particular for Sweden, Germany, and the Netherlands.

Minimal enrolment

Minimal enrolment requirements for community language teaching could be specified at the level of the class, the school, or even the municipality at large. The latter was common practice only in Sweden, and the minimal enrolment requirement there was five both for primary and secondary schools. All other countries were more reluctant, with minimal requirements for primary school pupils ranging from ten to twenty pupils (Germany, Belgium, France), or without any specification (the Netherlands and Spain). In the latter case, enrolment restrictions were commonly based on budget constraints.

Curricular status

In all countries, community language teaching at primary schools took place on a voluntary and optional basis, provided at the request of parents. Instruction took place within or outside regular school hours. The latter was most common in Sweden, Belgium, and France. Germany, the Netherlands (until 2004), and Spain allowed for two models of instruction, either within or outside regular school hours, depending on the type of language (in Germany), the type of goal (auxiliary or intrinsic in the Netherlands), and the type of organisation (in integrated or parallel classes in Spain). The number of community language teaching hours varied from one to five hours per week. If community language teaching took place at secondary schools, it was considered a regular and optional subject within school hours in all countries under consideration.

Funding

The funding of community language teaching depended on national, regional, or local educational authorities in the country or municipality of residence and/or on the consulates or embassies of the countries of origin. In the latter case, consulates or embassies commonly recruited and provided the teachers, and were also responsible for teacher (in-service) training. Funding through the country and/or municipality of residence took place in Sweden. Funding through the consulates/embassies of the countries of origin took place in Belgium and Spain. A mixed type of funding occurred in Germany and in France. In Germany, the source of funding was dependent on particular languages or organisational models for community language teaching. In France, source countries funded community language teaching in primary schools, whereas the French ministry of education funded community language teaching in secondary schools.

Teaching materials

Teaching materials for community language teaching originated from the countries of origin or of residence of the pupils. Funding from ministries, municipalities, and/or publishing houses occurred in Sweden, Germany, and the Netherlands, although limited resources were available. Source country funding for community language teaching occurred in Belgium and Spain. In France, source countries funded teaching materials in primary schools, whereas the French ministry of education funded teaching materials in secondary schools.

Teacher qualifications

Teacher qualifications for community language teaching depended on educational authorities in the countries of residence or of origin. National or state-wide (in-service) teacher training programmes for community language teaching at primary and/or secondary schools existed in Sweden, Germany, and the Netherlands, although the appeal of these programmes was limited, given the many uncertainties about community language teaching job perspectives. In Belgium and Spain, teacher qualifications depended on educational authorities in the countries of origin. France had a mixed system of responsibilities: source countries were responsible for teacher qualifications in primary schools, whereas the French ministry of education was responsible for teacher qualifications in secondary schools.

Conclusion

From this brief overview, it is clear that there were remarkable cross-national differences in the status of community language teaching. In the same vein, there were also considerable differences between primary and secondary education in the status of community language teaching. A comparison of all nine parameters revealed that community language teaching had gained a higher status in secondary schools than in primary schools. In primary education, community language teaching was generally not part of the regular or national curriculum, and, therefore, became a negotiable entity in a complex, and often opaque, interplay between a variety of actors. Another important difference was that, in some countries (in particular France, Belgium, Spain, and some German federal states), community language teaching was funded by the consulates or embassies of the countries of origin. In these cases, the national government did not interfere in the organisation of community language teaching, or in the requirements for teachers, or in teacher selection and employment. A paradoxical consequence of this phenomenon was that the earmarking of community language teaching budgets was often safeguarded by the above-mentioned consulates or embassies.

The higher status of community language teaching in secondary education was largely due to the fact that instruction in one or more languages, other than the national standard language, was a traditional and regular component of the (optional) school curriculum, whereas primary education was mainly determined by a monolingual *habitus* (Gogolin, 1994). *Within* secondary education, however, community language teaching had to compete with foreign languages that had a higher status or a longer tradition.

VALEUR: Valuing All Languages in Europe

Joanna McPake, Scottish CILT (Centre for Information on Language Teaching and Research)

The VALEUR project (2004-7) formed part of the Second Medium Term Programme of activities to support the implementation of Council of Europe languages education policies, sponsored by the European Centre for Modern Languages (ECML). The aim was to map provision for community language learning for children of school age across Europe. Experts from 21 Council of Europe states, ranging from Armenia to Iceland, participated in the project, collating information about the nature of provision in their own countries, and examples of good practice.

It was established that at least 440 spoken languages, from every inhabited continent, and at least eighteen sign languages were in use in participating states. Although these figures are almost certainly underestimates, as they are dependent on the extent to which data collection in each participating country is comprehensive and up to date, they represent a considerable advance on previous estimates (eg European Commission, 2006b). The community languages which were most widely spoken (ie found in the greatest number of states) were Polish and German (17 states); French, Arabic and Russian (16); Spanish and Turkish (15); Romani (14); English and Mandarin (13). This list of languages makes it clear that any language has the potential to be a community language, including the national languages of other European states, as well as languages from beyond Europe. The countries reporting the greatest number of community languages were the UK (288), Spain (198) and Ireland (158); but even countries with small populations reported that a range of community languages were spoken: for example, Latvia, with a population of 2.3 million people, reported 26 languages; Slovenia (2 million) reported 24 languages; and Estonia (1.3 million) reported eighteen languages in use.

The project also found that provision for learning these community languages was available for around a quarter (24%) of the total number of languages known to be in use: 97 spoken languages and 12 sign languages. Four key types of provision were identified: community languages used as media of instruction in schools; community languages taught as subjects during the school day; community languages taught after school hours; community languages in the context of intercultural education. Provision is very patchy, however; it is not necessarily the case that all those who would wish to study their community language have access to suitable provision, even when that language is listed as being taught somewhere in the country in which they live.

The project sought to identify good practice, defined as practice which is effective in ensuring that learners progress towards desired goals. Several factors were identified as critical: structures to support provision must be in place, and resources – including trained teachers and appropriate materials – need to be available; a systematic approach to recording learners' progression and attainment is required; in some circumstances, a commitment to the revitalisation of languages which have been suppressed and are at risk of dying out, and an understanding of how to undertake such initiatives, are crucial to success.

The full report of the VALEUR project is available from http://www.ecml.at/mtp2/VALEUR/html/A1_Valeur_reportE.pdf

Conclusion to Part 3

Reviewing the contributions in the final part of the book, we can see what factors constrain or enable the 'pedagogies of possibility' and 'policies of possibility' that we discussed in our overview. The considered action of teachers shines out strongly as one of the most important elements in planning for a multilingual future. The example of Arabic-Hebrew bilingual schools in Israel shows us that even in the most critical and difficult situations, teachers from different backgrounds can work together to forge visionary pedagogies. In this case, pedagogies are directly challenging the politics of separation.

Returning to Europe, language directives at European Union level seem to be moving in the direction of 'policies of possibility', with greater attention paid to regional and minority languages and the new goal of plurilingualism for all citizens. However, national or local policies turn out to be highly varied as to whether they support, restrict or ignore plurilingualism. Furthermore, policies can languish as rhetoric unless they are translated into action. Teachers therefore remain at the forefront in terms of constructing progressive pedagogies to meet the needs of learners in multilingual contexts.

For example, in the UK the National Languages Strategy officially promotes early language learning, yet a bilingual pre-school receives little support to extend its successful work to primary school level in a system that only recognises English as a medium of instruction. In Luxembourg, all schools operate trilingually but the state has yet to move to a plurilingual curriculum that addresses the languages of all its learners, so teachers are themselves finding ways for children to use their full repertoire of linguistic resources in the classroom. In Ireland, Irish is an official language but policy alone cannot overturn its societal status as a threatened indigenous language. English therefore continues to dominate in the lived experience of learners, even threatening to take over spaces officially dedicated to Irish such as immersion pre-schools. Teachers in Ireland need to reflect, re-evaluate and resist by de-

185

signing pedagogies that address the different needs of learners in order to maximise the use of Irish.

The key role played by teachers highlights the challenge for teacher education to address the continually changing needs of diverse multilingual populations. Both new and experienced teachers must be empowered to develop and explore inclusive practices, using conceptual frameworks and methodological tools based on rigorous research. Informed reflective practitioners can act at the interface between policy and learners and adapt their practices and pedagogies sensitively to local needs. This involves being able to analyse their own contexts critically, and go beyond them as both policy and practice evolve. We see examples of this in recent initiatives for training community language teachers and in new pedagogies for supporting bilingual learners in the UK.

In this demanding situation, collaboration between teacher educators and practitioners in different countries is vital in order to support one another and exchange ideas. The success of the international TESSLA project (Teacher Education for the Support of Second Language Acquisition) and teacher exchanges between the UK, France, Germany and Spain illustrate the rewards to be gained from such collaboration.

Similar collaboration is needed between policy makers across Europe, at both national and local level, to ensure that minority languages are being treated on an equal basis with dominant European languages. As the VALEUR project shows, an acceptance that all languages are valuable requires that all languages are supported and integrated into the overall European framework; this includes fragile indigenous languages such as Irish, Catalan and Luxembourgish as well as minority languages such as Urdu, Turkish or Somali. Assessment will play a significant role in determining the way forward in inclusive language education, so further moves need to be made towards recognising proficiency in minority languages – such as through the Languages Ladder scheme, which allows for recognition of achievement in a range of languages, not just in languages formerly considered desirable.

With support and recognition for all their languages, children from diverse language backgrounds are perfectly placed to become the plurilingual citizens sought by the European Union. Many of them can already use several different languages for different purposes, switching flexibly as required and paying attention to cultural appropriacy. 'Pedagogies of possibility' will enable them to build on these skills. Such pedagogies will also benefit all children by extending the range of languages available for learning and broadening the curriculum into new areas of intercultural understanding.

Discussion points

The following questions can be used to draw together ideas and information arising from the different contributions in Multilingual Europe: Diversity and Learning.

1. How do differences in the status of particular languages manifest themselves in contexts explored in this book?

2. How might children and young people become aware of differences in language status?

3. How do learner, family and teacher identities influence language learning and achievement?

4. What can parents and grandparents contribute to their children's linguistic and cultural development, and how can schools encourage that contribution?

5. What is the role of out-of-school learning, eg community classes, in language learning and identity formation?

6. How can schools work effectively with communities to foster language maintenance?

7. How can teacher education take account of linguistic and cultural diversity?

8. How can teachers from minority language backgrounds be involved in mainstream education, and what would the benefits be for learners?

9. How can community languages be included in assessment?

10. What role can European-level policies play in promoting plurilingualism and intercultural understanding?

11. What kinds of policies can states and cities produce in order to develop multilingualism in their citizens, and what are the benefits for them?

12. How can states that are maintaining threatened indigenous languages also offer support to new ones?

13. How can the world wide web play a role in creating virtual communities, eg among diasporic communities, among educators, children in schools, and language learners?

14. What kinds of multilingual initiatives bring people together across boundaries (geographical, linguistic, generational or political)?

References

Al-Haj, M. (2002) Multiculturalism in deeply divided societies: the Israeli case. *International Journal of Intercultural Relations* 26, 169-183

Amara, M. (2005) *The Bilingual Education Model of Hand-in-Hand* (in Hebrew). Jerusalem: Hand in Hand, Centre for Jewish-Arab Education in Israel

Amara, M. and Mari, A. (2002) *Language Education Policy: The Arab Minority in Israel.* Dordrecht, Netherlands: Kluwer Academic Publishing

Anderson, J. (forthcoming) Pre- and in-service professional development of teachers of community/ heritage languages in the UK: insider perspectives. *Language and Education*

Anderson, J., Kenner, C. and Gregory, E. (2008) The National Languages Strategy in the UK: are minority languages still on the margins? In C. Helot and A. De Mejia (eds) *Forging Multilingual Spaces: Integrating Perspectives on Majority and Minority Bilingual Education.* Clevedon: Multilingual Matters

Axelsson, M. (2005) Literacy events and literacy socialisation in Stockholm's multilingual pre-schools. In M. Axelsson, C. Rosander and M. Sellgren (eds) *Stärkta Trådar: Flerspråkiga Barn och Ungdomar Utvecklar Språk, Litteracitet och Kunskap (Strengthened Threads: Multilingual Children and Adolescents Develop Language, Literacy and Knowledge).* Stockholm: Rinkeby Institute of Multilingual Research

Baker, C. (2006) *Foundations of Bilingual Education and Bilingualism (4th edition).* Clevedon: Multilingual Matters

Baker, C. and Jones, S. (1998) *Encyclopaedia of Bilingualism and Bilingual Education.* Clevedon, Avon: Multilingual Matters

Bakhtin, M. M. (1981) *The Dialogic Imagination: Four Essays.* Austin: University of Texas Press

Barradas, O. (2004) Portuguese students in London schools: Patterns of participation in community language classes and patterns of educational achievement. Unpublished PhD thesis, Goldsmiths, University of London

Barradas, O. (2007) Learning Portuguese: A tale of two worlds. In J. Conteh, P. Martin and L.H. Robertson (eds) *Multilingual Learning: Stories from Schools and Communities in Britain.* Stoke-on-Trent: Trentham

Barton, D. and Hamilton, M. (1998) *Local Literacies.* London: Routledge

BBC News (2006) Schools 'ignored' languages edict. November 1. http://news.bbc.co.uk/go/pr/fr/-/1/hi/education/6442837.stm (Accessed June 2008)

BBC (2007) *Schools to Get £50m Language Help* http://news.bbc.co.uk/go/pr/fr/-/1/hi/education/6442837.stm, Broadcast 12 March 2007

Beacco, J-C. and Byram, M. (2003) *From Linguistic Diversity to Plurilingual Education: Guide for the Development of Language Policies in Europe.* Strasbourg: Council of Europe

Bekerman, Z. and Shhadi, N. (2003) Palestinian-Jewish bilingual education in Israel: Its influence on cultural identities and its impact on inter-group conflict. *Journal of Multilingual and Multicultural Development* 24 (6), 473-484

Bell, A. (2001) Children's literature and international identity. In M. Meek (ed) *Children's Literature and National Identity.* Stoke on Trent: Trentham

Benavot, A. and Resh, N. (2003) Education governance, school autonomy, and curriculum implementation: A comparative study of Arab and Jewish schools in Israel. *Curriculum Studies* 35 (2), 171-196

Bénisti, A. (2004) *Rapport Préliminaire de la Commission Prévention du Groupe d'Études Parlementaire sur la Sécurité Intérieure, sur la Prévention de la Délinquence.* http://cirdel.lyon. free. fr/IMG/pdf/rapport_BENISTI_prevention.pdf (accessed 10/03/08)

Bhabha, H. (1994) *The Location of Culture.* London: Routledge

Bhavnani, K. and Phoenix, A. (1994) Shifting identities, shifting racisms: An introduction. *Feminism and Psychology* 4 (1), 5-18

Bourdieu, P. (1991) *Language and Symbolic Power.* Cambridge, MA: Harvard University Press

Boykin, W. (1994) Harvesting talent and culture: African-American children and educational reform. In R.Rossi (ed) *Schools and Students at Risk.* New York: Teachers College Press

Bruner, J. (1982) What is representation? In M. Roberts and J. Tamburrini (eds) *Child Development 0-5.* Edinburgh: Holmes McDougall

Bush, P. (2001) Towards a European policy on literary translation. *In Other Words* 17, 34-39

Callender, C. (1997) *Education For Empowerment: The Practice and Philosophies of Black Teachers.* Stoke-on-Trent: Trentham

Carrasco, S. (ed) (2004) *Inmigración, Contexto Familiar y Educación.* Barcelona: UAB

Carrasco, S. and Soto, P. (2003) *Immigració i diversitat cultural a les escoles de Barcelona.* Barcelona: Ajuntament de Barcelona

Castells, M. (2001) *The Power of Identity.* Oxford: Blackwell

Chatterjee, D. (2001) *Who Cares? Reminiscences of Yemeni Carers in Sheffield.* Sheffield: Yemeni Carers Project

Chen, Y. (2007) Contributing to success: Chinese parents and the community school. In J. Conteh, P. Martin and L.H. Robertson (eds) *Multilingual Learning: Stories from Schools and Communities in Britain.* Stoke-on-Trent: Trentham

CILT, The National Centre for Languages (2005) *Community Language Learning in England, Wales and Scotland.* London: CILT

CILT, The National Centre for Languages (2006) *Positively Plurilingual: The Contribution of Community Languages to UK Education and Society.* London: CILT

CILT, The National Centre for Languages (2007) *Curriculum Guide for Arabic* (by S. Saffaf and N. Abdel-Hay), *for Chinese* (by A. Thompson, E. Lee and K. Li), *for Panjabi* (by N. Chandla and P. Grewal), *for Tamil* (by S. Pillai and K. Nithiya), *for Urdu* (by K. Ali and H. Syed). London: CILT

CILT/NACELL (2006) *Primary Languages Training Manual.* London: CILT

Cole, M. (1985) The zone of proximal development: Where culture and cognition create each other. In J. V. Wertsch (ed) *Culture, Communication and Cognition: Vygotskyan Perspectives.* New York: Cambridge University Press

Cole, M. (1996) *Cultural Psychology: A Once and Future Discipline.* Cambridge, MA: Harvard University Press

Conteh, J. (2007a) Opening doors to success in multilingual classrooms: Bilingualism, codeswitching and the professional identities of 'ethnic minority' primary teachers. *Language and Education* 21 (6), 457-472

Conteh, J. (2007b) Bilingualism in mainstream primary classrooms in England. In Z. Hua, P. Seed-house, L. Wei, and V. Cook, (eds) *Language Learning and Teaching as Social Interaction.* London: Palgrave Macmillan

Conteh, J. (2007c) Culture, languages and learning: Mediating a 'bilingual approach' in comple-mentary Saturday classes. In J. Conteh, P. Martin and L.H. Robertson (eds) *Multilingual Learning: Stories from Schools and Communities in Britain.* Stoke-on-Trent: Trentham

Council of Europe (1992) *European Charter for Regional or Minority Languages.* http://conventions. coe.int/treaty/en/Treaties/Word/148.doc (Accessed June 2008)

Council of Europe (2000) *The Language Portfolio. Language Passport.* http://www.coe.int/T/DG4/ Portfolio/documents/Pass_2spr.pdf (Accessed June 2008)

Council of Europe (2001) *Common European Framework of Reference for Languages: Learning, Teaching, Assessment.* Strasbourg: Council of Europe http://www.coe.int/t/dg4/linguistic/Source/ Framework_EN.pdf (Accessed January 2008)

Council of Europe (2008) Ireland: Language Education Policy Profile 2005-2007. Strasbourg: Council of Europe http://www.coe.int/t/dg4/linguistic/Source/Profile%20Ireland_%20final_EN.doc (Accessed June 2008)

Coyle, D. (2000) Meeting the challenge: Developing the 3Cs curriculum. In S. Green (ed) *New Perspectives on Teaching and Learning Modern Languages.* Clevedon: Multilingual Matters

Craft, A. (2005) *Creativity in Schools: Tensions and Dilemmas.* London: Routledge

Creese, A. and Martin, P. (2003) Multilingual classroom ecologies: Inter-relationships, interactions and ideologies. *Bilingual Education and Bilingualism* 6 (3), 161-167

Crystal, D. (1997) *English as a Global Language.* Cambridge: Cambridge University Press

Cummins, J. (2001) *Negotiating Identities: Education for Empowerment in a Diverse Society.* Los Angeles, CA: California Association for Bilingual Education for the Ontario Institute for Studies in Education

Cummins, J. (2008) From compound and coordinate bilingualism to multicompetence and multi-literacies: Challenging dogma or embracing heresies? Paper presented at International conference on Language Issues in English-Medium Universities: A Global Concern 18-20 June 2008, Univer-sity of Hong Kong. http://www.hku.hk/clear/conference08/cummins.html#top (Accessed June 2008)

Datta, M. (2000) *Bilinguality and Literacy: Principles and Practice.* London: Continuum

Dearing, R. and King, L. (2006) *The Languages Review Consultation Report.* Annesley, Notts: DfES http://www.dfes.gov.uk/consultations/downloadableDocs/6869-DfES-Language%20Review. pdf (Accessed January 2008)

Debbasch, R. (2006) *Le directeur général de l'enseignement scolaire, pour le ministre de l'éduca-tion nationale, de l'enseignement supérieur et de la recherche et par delegation.* http://www. education.gouv.fr/bo/2006/31/MENE0602215C.htm (Accessed February 2008)

DES (Department of Education and Science) (1985) *Education for All. The Swann Report.* London: HMSO

DfEE (Department for Education and Employment) (1999) *All Our Futures: Creativity, Culture and Education.* London: DfEE

DfEE/QCA (Department for Education and Employment / Qualifications and Curriculum Authority) (1999) *Modern Foreign Languages: The National Curriculum for England.* London: HMSO

DfES (Department for Education and Skills) (2002a) *Green Paper, 14-19: Extending Opportunities, Raising Standards.* Annesley, Notts: DfES

DfES (Department for Education and Skills) (2002b) *Languages for All: Languages for Life. A Strategy for England.* Annesley, Notts: DfES, DFES/0749/2002. www.dfes.gov.uk/languages strategy. A progress report on the Strategy is published as Languages for all: from strategy to delivery. Annesley, Notts: DfES, 2004. ISBN: 1 84478 247 6. www.dfes.gov.uk/languages/DSP_nationallanguages_strategy.cfm (Accessed January 2008)

DfES (Department for Education and Skills) (2005) *The Key Stage 2 Framework for Languages.* Annesley, Notts: DfES

DfES (Department for Education and Skills) (2005) *The Languages Ladder.* Annesley, Notts: DfES www.teachernet.gov.uk/languagesladder. (Accessed January 2008)

DfES (Department for Education and Skills) (2007a) *Early Years Foundation Stage.* London: DfES

DfES (Department for Education and Skills) (2007b) *Languages Review.* Annesley, Notts: DfES

Desforges, C. and Abouchaar, A. (2003) *The Impact of Parental Involvement, Parental Support and Family Education on Pupil Achievement and Adjustment.* London: DfES

Dörnyei, Z. (2001) *Teaching and Researching Motivation.* London: Longman

EEC (European Economic Community) (1977) *Council Directive on the Education of Children of Migrant Workers.* 77/486/EEC

Edelenbos, P., Johnstone, R. and Kubanek, A. (2006) *Pedagogical Principles underlying the Teaching of Languages to Very Young Learners. Languages for the Children of Europe: Published Research, Good Practice and Main Principles.* Brussels: European Commission

Education Bradford (2004) *Policy on Multilingualism.* Bradford: Education Bradford

Eduscol (2007) *Les horaires et les programmes de l'école primaire, BO hors-série no. 5 du 12 avril 2007.* http://eduscol.education.fr/D0048/primprog.htm (Accessed February 2008)

Edwards, V. (2004) *Multilingualism in the English-speaking World.* Oxford: Blackwell

Engeström, Y., Miettinen, R. and Punamaki, R. (eds) (1999) *Perspectives on Activity Theory.* New York: Cambridge University Press

Erikson, T. (2006) Nations in cyberspace. http://www.tamilnation.org/selfdetermination/nation/erikson.htm (Accessed April.2007)

European Commission (1996). *Teaching and Learning – Towards the Learning Society.* COM (95) 590 final. Brussels: European Commission http://aei.pitt.edu/1132/01/education_train_wp_COM_95_590.pdf (Accessed January 2008)

European Commission (2003) *Promoting Language Learning and Linguistic Diversity. An Action Plan 2004-2006.* COM(2003) 449 final. Brussels: European Commission http://ec.europa.eu/education/doc/official/keydoc/actlang/act_lang_en.pdf (Accessed June 2008)

European Commission (2004) *Many Tongues, One Family: Languages in the European Union.* July 2004. Brussels: European Commission http://europa.eu.int/comm/publications/booklets/move/45/en.doc (Accessed June 2008)

European Commission (2005) *A New Framework Strategy for Multilingualism.* COM(2005) 596 final. Brussels: European Commission http://europa.eu/languages/servlets/Doc?id=913 (Accessed January 2008)

European Commission (2006a) *Lifelong Learning Programme 2007-2013.* Brussels: European Commission http://ec.europa.eu/education/programmes/llp/index_en.html (Accessed January 2008)

European Commission (2006b) *Special Eurobarometer. Europeans and their Languages.* Brussels: European Commission http://ec.europa.eu/public_opinion/archives/ebs/ebs_243_en.pdf. (Accessed June 2008)

European Commission (2007) *Report on the Implementation of the Action Plan 'Promoting Language Learning and Linguistic Diversity'.* COM(2007) 554 final. Brussels: European Commission http://ec.europa.eu/education/policies/lang/doc/com554_en.pdf (Accessed June 2008)

REFERENCES

European Union (2000) *Charter of Fundamental Rights of the European Union. Article 22. Official Journal of the European Communities 364/5, 18.12.2000 p1.* Brussels: European Parliament http://www.europarl.europa.eu/charter/pdf/text_en.pdf (Accessed January 2008)

Eurydice (2005) *Key Data on Teaching Languages at School in Europe.* http://www.eurydice.org/Documents/KDLANG/2005/EN/FrameSet.htm (Accessed June 2008)

Extra, G. and Verhoeven, L. (eds) (1998) *Bilingualism and Migration.* Berlin: Mouton De Gruyter

Extra, G. and Yagmur, K. (eds) (2002) *Language Diversity in Multicultural Europe: Comparative Perspectives on Immigrant Minority Languages at Home and at School.* Paris: UNESCO http://www.unesco.org/most/dp63extra.pdf (accessed June 2008)

Extra, G. and Yagmur, K. (eds) (2004) *Urban Multilingualism in Europe: Immigrant Minority Languages at Home and School.* Clevedon: Multilingual Matters

Feuerverger, G. (2001) *Oasis of Dreams: Teaching and Learning Peace in a Jewish-Palestinian Village in Israel.* New York: Routledge

Francis, B. and Archer, L. (2005) British-Chinese pupils' constructions of the value of education. *British Educational Research Journal* 31 (1), 89-103

Freire, P. (1990) *Pedagogy of the Oppressed.* New York: Seabury Press

Freire, P. and Macedo, D. (1987) *Literacy: Reading the Word and the World.* London: Bergin and Garvey

Gillborn, D. and Gipps, C. (1996) *Recent Research on the Achievements of Minority Ethnic Pupils.* London: HMSO

Gogolin, I. (1994) *Der Monolinguale Habitus der Multilingualen Schule.* Münster/New York: Waxmann

González, N., Moll, L. and Amanti, C. (2005) *Funds of Knowledge: Theorizing Practices in Households, Communities and Classrooms.* Mahwah, New Jersey: Erlbaum

Graddol D. (2006) *English Next.* London: British Council

Gregory, E. (1996) *Making Sense of a New World: Learning to Read in a Second Language.* London: Paul Chapman

Gregory, E. (2001) Sisters and brothers as language and literacy teachers: Synergy between siblings playing and working together. *Journal of Early Childhood Literacy* 1 (3), 301-22

Gregory, E., Arju, T., Jessel, J., Kenner, C. and Ruby, M. (2007) Snow White in different guises: Interlingual and intercultural exchanges between grandparents and young children at home in East London. *Journal of Early Childhood Literacy* 7 (1), 5-25

Gregory, E., Long, S. and Volk, D. (eds) (2004) *Many Pathways to Literacy: Young Children Learning with Siblings, Grandparents, Peers and Communities.* London: RoutledgeFalmer

Hall, D. (2001) *Assessing the Needs of Bilingual Pupils: Living in Two Languages (2nd edition).* London: David Fulton

Halliday, F. (1992) *Arabs in Exile.* London: Tauris and Co Ltd

Hancock, A., Hermeling, S., Landon, J. and Young, A. (2006) *Building on Diversity with Young Children: Teacher Education for the Support of Second Language Acquisition.* Berlin : LIT Verlag

Harrigan, P. (1999) *Report to the High-Level Committee of the Tamil Virtual University.* http://www.xlweb.com/heritage/asian/tvu_report.htm#extant (Accessed April 2007)

Heath, S.B. (1983) *Ways with Words.* Cambridge: Cambridge University Press

Heller, M. (1995) Language choice, social institutions, and symbolic domination. *Language in Society* 24, 373-405

Hélot, C. (2002) Crossing the boundaries of language and culture through reading, writing, and playing. In C. Hélot and I. Tsamadou-Jacoberger (eds) *Intercultural Education and the Translation of Children's Literature*. Strasbourg: Presses de l'Université Marc Bloch de Strasbourg/IUFM

Hélot, C. (2005) Bridging the gap between prestigious bilingualism and the bilingualism of minorities: towards an integrated perspective of multilingualism in the French education context. In M. Ó'Laire (ed) *Multilingualism in Educational Settings*. Tübingen: Stauffenburg Verlag

Hélot, C. (2007) *Du Bilinguisme en Famille au Plurilinguisme à l'École*. Paris: L'Harmattan

Hélot, C. and Young, A. S. (2006) Imagining multilingual education in France: A language and cultural awareness project at primary level. In T. Skutnabb-Kangas, O. Garcia, and M.E. Torres Guzman (eds) *Imagining Multilingual Schools*. Clevedon: Multilingual Matters

Hickey, T. (1997) *Early Immersion Education in Ireland: Na Naíonraí/An Luath-Thumadh in Éirinn: Na Naíonraí*. Baile Átha Cliath: ITÉ. http://www.eric.ed.gov/ERICDocs/data/ericdocs2sql/content_storage_01/0000019b/80/15/65/86.pdf (Accessed June 2008)

Hickey, T. (2001) Mixing beginners and native speakers in Irish immersion: Who is immersing whom? *Canadian Modern Language Review* 57 (3), 443-474 http://www.utpjournals.com/jour.ihtml?lp=product/cmlr/573/573-Hickey.html (Accessed June 2008)

Hickey, T. (2007) Children's language networks in minority language immersion: What goes in may not come out. *Language and Education* 21 (1), 46-65

Holland, D. and Lave, J. (2001) *History in Person: Enduring Struggles, Contentious Practices, Intimate Identities*. Santa Fe, New Mexico: SAR Press

Hornberger, N.H. (ed.) (2003). *Continua of Biliteracy: An Ecological Framework for Educational Policy, Research, and Practice in Multilingual Settings*. Clevedon: Multilingual Matters

Horner, K. and Weber, J.J. (2008) The language situation in Luxembourg. *Current Issues in Language Planning* 9 (1), 69-128

James, T. (2000) *Kurt Hahn and the Aims of Education*. http://www.kurthahn.org/writings/james.pdf (Accessed June 2008)

Jessel, J., Arju, T., Gregory, E., Kenner, C. and Ruby, M. (2004) Children and their grandparents at home: A mutually supportive context for learning and linguistic development. *English Quarterly* 36 (4), 16-23

Johnstone, R. (2001) *Immersion in a Second or Additional Language at School: Evidence from International Research*. Report for the Scottish Executive Education Department. http://www.scilt.stir.ac.uk/publications/ (Accessed June 2008)

Junyent, C. (2004) *Veus, Voices, Voces, Voix*. Barcelona: Lunwerg

Kenner, C. (2004) *Becoming Biliterate: Young Children Learning Different Writing Systems*. Stoke-on-Trent: Trentham Books

Kenner, C., Ruby, M., Gregory, E., Jessel, J. and Arju, T. (2007) Intergenerational learning between children and grandparents in East London. *Journal of Early Childhood Research* 5 (2), 219-243

Kenner, C., Gregory, E., Ruby, M. and Al-Azami, S. (2008) Bilingual learning for second and third generation children. *Language, Culture and Curriculum* 21 (2), 120-137

King, L. and Johnstone, R. (2001) *An Agenda for Languages*. Report produced by CILT for the Birmingham Conference of October 2001. London: CILT http://www.eyl2001.org.uk/agenda.pdf (Accessed January 2008)

Lave, J. and Wenger, E. (1991) *Situated Learning: Legitimate Peripheral Participation*. Cambridge: Cambridge University Press

Läroplan för förskolan Lpfö 98 (1998) Stockholm: Fritzes

Lewis, E. (1981) *Bilingualism and Bilingual Education*. Oxford: Pergamon Press

MEN (2006) http://www.education.gouv.fr/cid2659/les-parents.html (Accessed February 2008)

McPake, J. (2006) *Provision for Community Language Learning in Scotland: Final Report.* http://www.scotland.gov.uk/Publications/2006/09/07093013/0 (Accessed June 2008)

McPake, J., Tinsley, T., Broeder, P., Mijares, L., Latomoaa, S. and Martyniuk, W. (2007) *Valuing All Languages in Europe.* European Centre for Modern Languages, Graz: Council of Europe Publishing

McPake, J., Tinsley, T. and James, C. (2007) Making provision for community languages: Issues for teacher education in the UK. *Language Learning Journal* 35 (1), 99-112

Marsh, D. (ed) (2002) *CLIL/EMILE – The European Dimension: Actions, Trends and Foresight Potential.* University of Jyväskylä, Finland: UniCOM http://europa.eu.int/comm/education/policies/lang/doc/david_marsh-report.pdf (Accessed January 2007)

Maurer, M.P., Fixmer, P. and Boualam, R. (2007) Language uses in the family contexts of 3 to 9 year old children in Luxembourg. Unpublished draft report, University of Luxembourg

Max, C., Portante, D. and Stammet, B. (2005) Literacy learning in three languages. Paper presented at the Dissemination Conference for the Multilingual Europe ESRC seminar series at Goldsmiths, University of London, November 12, 2005

Meinhof, U. H. and Galasinski, D. (2005) *The Language of Belonging.* Hampshire, UK: Palgrave

Mills, J. (2005) Connecting communities: Identity, language, diaspora. *International Journal of Bilingual Education and Bilingualism* 8 (4), 253-274

Ministerial Action Group on Languages (2000) *Citizens of a Multilingual World.* Edinburgh: Scottish Executive http://www.scotland.gov.uk/library3/education/mwki-00.asp (Accessed January 2008)

Moll, L.C., Amanti, C., Neff, D. and González, N. (1992) Funds of knowledge for teaching: using a qualitative approach to connect homes and classrooms. *Theory into Practice* 31 (2), 132-141

Mor-Sommerfeld, A. (2005) Bilingual education in areas of conflict – bridging and sharing. *Race Equality Teaching* 24 (1), 31-42

Mor-Sommerfeld, A., Azaiza, F. and Hertz-Lazarowitz, R. (2007) Into the future: Towards bilingual education in Israel. *Education, Citizenship and Social Justice* 2(1), 5-22

NACELL (2007) *Initial Teacher Training Courses.* www.nacell.org.uk/profdev/itt.htm

Nieto, S. (1999) *The Light in Their Eyes: Creating Multicultural Learning Communities.* Stoke-on-Trent: Trentham

Nuffield Languages Inquiry (2000) *Languages: The Next Generation.* London: The Nuffield Foundation

Pillai, S. and Nithiya, K. (2007) *Curriculum Guide for Tamil.* London: CILT, The National Centre for Languages

Portante, D. (2004) Developing multilingual literacy in a complex setting: suggested principles for building a crossnational research agenda. http://www.readingonline.org/international/edinburgh/portante/

Portante, D., Arend, B., Boualam, R., Fixmer, P., Max. C., Elcheroth, S., Maurer-Hetto, M.P., Roth-Dury, E. and Sunnen, P. (2007) Children's plurilingualism up to the age of 9: Linguistic diversity, learning Luxembourgish and emergent literacies. Unpublished final report, University of Luxembourg and National Research Fund, Luxembourg

Prost, A. (2006) *L'enfant enjeu historique d'une longue suspicion.* In *Le Monde de l'Éducation,* March 2006

Razfar, A., and Gutiérrez, K. (2003) Reconceptualizing early childhood literacy: The sociocultural influence. In N. Hall, J. Larson and J. Marsh (eds) *Handbook of Early Childhood Literacy.* London: Sage

Rogoff, B. (1990) *Apprenticeship in Thinking.* New York: Oxford University Press

Rogoff, B. (2003) *The Cultural Nature of Human Development.* New York: Oxford University Press

Ruby, M., Kenner, C., Jessel, J., Gregory, E. and Arju, T. (2007) Gardening with grandparents: An early engagement with the science curriculum. *Early Years* 27 (2), 131-144

Sivasupramaniam, V. (2004) History of the Tamil diaspora. http://murugan.org/research/sivasupramaniam.htm (Accessed April 2007)

Smithers, R. and Whitford, B. (2006) 'Free fall' fears as pupils abandon languages. *Education Guardian.* August 25. http://www.guardian.co.uk/uk/2006/aug/25/gcses.topstories3 (Accessed June 2008)

Sterne, H.H. (1964) A foreign language in the primary school? Paper presented to the International Conference on Modern Language Teaching, Berlin

Tabouret-Keller, A. (1998) Language and identity. In F. Coulmas (ed) *The Handbook of Socio-linguistics.* Oxford: Blackwell

Tapscott, D. (1998) *Growing Up Digital: The Rise of the Net Generation.* New York: McGraw-Hill

Teacher Training Agency (2002) *Qualifying to Teach: Professional Standards for Qualified Teacher Status and Requirements for Initial Teacher Training.* London: TTA

Training and Development Agency for Schools (2007b) *Common Reference Framework – Anglo/French* http://www.tda.gov.uk/upload/resources/pdf/c/common_reference_framework.pdf (Accessed June 2008)

Valdés, G. (1997) Dual-language immersion programs: A cautionary note concerning the education of language-minority students. *Harvard Educational Review* 67 (3), 391-42

Vygotsky, L. (1978) *Mind in Society.* Cambridge, Mass: Harvard University Press

Welsh Assembly Government (2002) *Languages Count: The Welsh Assembly Government's National Modern Foreign Languages Strategy.* Cardiff: Welsh Assembly Government http://new.wales.gov.uk/docrepos/40382/4038232/4038211/4038293/languagescount-e.pdf?lang=en

Wenger, E. (1998) *Communities of Practice. Learning, Meaning and Identity.* Cambridge: Cambridge University Press

Williams, C. (2000) Bilingual teaching and language distribution at 16+. *International Journal of Bilingual Education and Bilingualism*, 3 (2), 129-48

Williams, K. (2000) Why teach foreign languages in schools? *Impact* No. 5. London: Philosophy of Education Society of Great Britain

Woodward, K. (2002) *Understanding Identity.* London: Arnold

Young, A. S. (2007) Diversity as an asset: Multiple language integration. In M. Dooly and D. Eastment (eds) *How We're Going About It: Teachers' Voices on Innovative Approaches to Teaching and Learning Languages.* Newcastle upon Tyne: Cambridge Scholars Publishing

Young, A. S. and Helot, C. (2007) Parent power: Parents as a linguistic and cultural resource at school. In A. Camilleri Grima (ed) *Promoting Linguistic Diversity and Whole-School Development.* Strasbourg, Council of Europe/ECML (European Centre for Modern Languages)

Index